D1457240

Cover Design

Cover Art. 2008 four- panel Advent Banner for the AMBS Chapel of the Sermon on the Mount (inspired by Vincent Van Gogh's "Starry Night"). Each panel is 80 x 27 inches, made with acrylic paint on Roc-Lon fabric. Artist: Rosanna Eller McFadden, Minister of Worship Arts at Creekside Church of the Brethren, Elkhart, IN (AMBS MDiv, 2011; used with permission). Photography credit and cover design: Mary Klassen, AMBS Director of Communications. Cover design and layout: Darin Simms, Evangel Publishing.

John's Gospel, lacking the Advent nativity stories, boldly introduces the Word as Creator of life and light: "we beheld his glory, full of grace and truth." The light of divine glory pervades the Gospel. Each of the four banners reveals more fully God's glory light, as does Jesus, "the light of the world." As in John's Gospel, so in this banner the fullness of glory-light bursts into a cross-resurrection image.

i

In *Living Gift*, we receive the rare gift of intimate glimpses into the mind and heart of a devoted biblical scholar as he engages personally with scripture. Professor Swartley shares the music, poetry, drama, and visual art that illuminated and inspired his study of John's Gospel. All who follow his example of integrating the mind and heart in scripture study will reap similar rewards of insight, conviction, wonder and joy.

-Marlene Kropf, recently retired, former Denominational Minister of Worship for Mennonite Church USA; Associate Professor of Spiritual Formation and Worship at AMBS in Elkhart, Indiana

John's Gospel beautifully illustrates how the God of the Universe is incarnated to humanity: heaven kisses earth in the person of Jesus Christ. In that spirit, Willard Swartley provides a holistic devotional companion to his commentary, *John*. Where many devotionals can divorce mind from heart (or vice-versa), *Living Gift* helps readers incarnate the *logos* of John's Gospel by engaging the full person (heart, soul, mind and strength) in the wonder and awe of John's Gospel.

-Rev. Jason Barnhart, Director of Denominational Advancement, The Brethren Church, Ashland, Ohio

Living Gift is a true gift. So many times we are offered great scholarly works, but we are left on our own to experience…to feel the text. Other literary works provide tools for spiritual formation, but lack the historical and cultural context of the biblical passage. *Living Gift* is rich precisely because it offers both. It blends mind and heart. Swartley helps us see we cannot truly understand the theological significance of John without also allowing Jesus of whom he writes to dwell within us.

-Michelle Hershberger
Bible teacher at Hesston College, KS

Biblical study, especially in service of worship and preaching, often focuses on distilling truth cognitively. Yet the church has a long history of reading the text not just with the mind, but with the senses, with touch and smell, sight and sound. With this companion to his *John* commentary, Swartley helps us recover these ways of reading, and of teaching and preaching. This book will serve Christians in private study, Sunday School classes, small groups, and spiritual direction groups in group study, and preachers in the preparation of sermons.

-Phil Waite, Pastor
College Mennonite Church, Goshen, IN

This marvelous work by Willard Swartley blends spiritual truth in its historical context with artistic expression in manner that is both creative and useful. Willard begins each Gospel portion with insightful nuggets that set the stage. These are then expanded with the inclusion of meditations, poetry, song, art, and/or responsive readings that bring out the meaning and significance of the text. This will be a valuable tool in the hands of worship leaders, worship committees, pastors, and those who seek to bask in the beauty as well as experience the impact of the message of love and salvation portrayed by this Gospel.

-Larry Diener, Minister of Worship
Bahia Vista Mennonite Church, Sarasota, FL

This is a rich resource for worship planners, leaders, and pastors, and helpful as well for personal reflection. It is part commentary with nuggets of information and insight centered on John's Gospel, with art, prayers, poetry, stories, drama dialogues, hymn texts, and much more that spark the spiritual imagination.

-April Yamasaki, lead pastor, Emmanuel Mennonite, Abbotsford, B.C.
Author of *Sacred Pauses: Spiritual Practices for Personal Renewal*

Living Gift is a gentle and inspirational book, artistically-sensitive and insightful, caring about the life of the soul. Knowing Willard, this is no surprise. It may be used in order from beginning to end, or selectively. The suggestions Swartley offers for personal reflections and the indices at the end of the book are useful in making the book one's own.

-Ken Nafziger, Professor of Music at Eastern Mennonite University
Actively engaged in hymn singing and worship activities
in Mennonite and other denominational circles

Willard Swartley's thought-provoking, meditative treatment of John's Gospel is itself a gift. It is rich in suggestions for spiritual reflection through poetry, music, visual arts, prayer and litany. As a companion to his commentary on John's Gospel, this is a delightful, inspirational read, filled with the Spirit and flowing with grace and peace.

-Carol Spicher Waggy, Interim District Executive Minister
Northern Indiana District, Church of the Brethren

This is a wonderfully creative, unique companion to Swartley's BCBC Commentary on John (Herald Press, 2013). It enables the message of the Fourth Gospel to penetrate and impact not only the mind, but the heart as well. With both the commentary and this companion piece we have exposition on the Fourth Gospel that perceives the task at hand is more than right understanding. It matches the Gospel's purpose: to call people to encounter the Word made flesh and to abide in that Word.

- Jeff T. Williams, Pastor of the Nappanee Brethren in Christ Church

Living Gift:

John's Jesus in Meditation and Poetry,

Art and Song

Willard Swartley

Willard Swartley
Thanksgiving 2013

Evangel
Publishing House
Nappanee, Indiana 46550

ISBN-13: 978-1-934233-33-7
Library of Congress Control Number: 2013904231
Printed in the United States of America
13 14 15 16 EP 8 7 6 5 4 3 2 1

Dedicated to all my helpers

especially my Gospel of John students

and Mary

in the making of this book

Contents (for **Figures**, listing Art Images, see the Index, p.163)

Introduction		1
John 1:1-18	John's Gospel Prologue	7
John 1:19–2:12	A Week of New Creation	17
John 2:13–4:3	From Old to New: Temple, Birth, Baptism	21
John 4:4-54	Jesus' Peace-Mission into Samaria: Savior of the World	31
John 5	Jesus Works God's Work; "Trial" Begins	39
John 6	Jesus: I am the Bread of Life	41
John 7	Jesus: Living Water, at the Feast of Tabernacles	47
John 8	Truth on Trial: Jesus and the Pharisees-"The Jews"	51
John 9	Blindness and Sight: Who Is Jesus?	55
John 10	Jesus: I am the Good Shepherd	69
John 11:1–12:11	Jesus' Climactic Sign: Lazarus's Death, Resurrection, and Aftermath	73
John 12:12-50	The Final Scene in Jesus' Public Ministry	79
John 13:1-38	Jesus Begins "Farewell"	85
John 13:35–16:33	Overview of Jesus' Farewell Discourse	93
John 14:1–31	Jesus' Love; The Way, The Truth, and The Life	97
John 15:1–16:4	Mutual Indwelling of Jesus and Disciples: Abiding and Loving, Facing Hatred	101
John 16:5-33	The Work of the Paraclete; Jesus' Departure and Consolation: Joy and Peace	109
John 17:1-26	Jesus Prays to His Father	113
John 18:1-27	Jesus' Arrest, Jewish Trial, and Peter's Denials	123
John 18:28–19:42	Jesus' Trial before Pilate, Death, and Burial	125
John 20	Risen Jesus Ignites Mission and New Community	131
John 21	New Horizons and Destinies	141
Sermon on Peter (Author)		143
Antiphon on Word and I AM (Jim and Sally Longley)		148
Spiritual Reflection		152
Blessing and Sending		153
Art "Journey" (Kris A. Shenk).		154
Bibliography		155
Indexes (Author, Genres, Subject by Genres)		159
Acknowledgments		181
Author Bio		183

Introduction

John's Gospel over the centuries has generated much poetry and music of the soul. John's Gospel is a work of art. Because John is pervasively symbolic, with rich imagery, it borders on the mystical, though ever grounded in the historical and political. This volume of meditations, poetry, art, and song complements the Believers Church Bible Commentary (Herald Press) on John's Gospel, which I authored. This book appropriates the Gospel to aid spiritual formation, so that Jesus indwells us more fully. Its purpose is to nourish the spirit and bring light, life, and love to bloom within us.

The Gospel of John's grip on my soul goes back to the late sixties when my first doctoral dissertation proposal at Princeton Theological Seminary was on John's Gospel, and specifically its distinctive epistemology of love, love as a way of knowing. Love knows God's heart, and God's heart in and through Jesus is unveiled to us in love, from creation to cross-glorification to resurrection-exaltation, with "Peace be with you" as Jesus' own signature.

As we open our spirit to the Gospel's fascinating narrative, it bears the fruit of meditation, poetry, art, and song. Just as Jesus *must* go through Samaria, so the Gospel *must* move into the heart, with this unique narrative centered on the true Jesus-Vine to bear spiritual fruit. May this book aid your spiritual formation and draw you to Jesus, who as the "lifted up" Son of Man and Son of God draws all people, Jews and Gentiles, to himself and God.

John's Gospel vies with Mark as my favorite. Both have narratives with "suspense" at their compositional heart. For Mark it is the unfolding *mystery* (Greek, *mystērion*). In John we encounter a similar literary technique: the *hour has not*/then suddenly *has come*. John is more subtle and complex than Mark in interweaving numerous crucial themes, from its distinctive Christology with its many titles for Jesus and Father-Son union to a politically powerful passion narrative, with Jesus facing down Pilate in extended dialogue.

The matter of the Gospel's authorship deepens its mystery. While tradition assigns it to John the Apostle and/or John the Elder, both located at Ephesus in the 90s AD, scholarship of the last century has proposed other options, of which Lazarus is a candidate. Why so? The Gospel associates authorship with the Beloved Disciple (13:23; 19:35; 20:2; 21:7, 23-24) whose identity is most mysterious. John 11:3, 5 introduces Lazarus as the disciple Jesus loved. Perhaps *he* is the bearer of the tradition that later clusters around the community endeared to John the Apostle. Or maybe there is some connection between Lazarus, the

1

Jerusalem disciple who is eye-witness to the many Jerusalem events of the Gospel, and John the Elder at Ephesus.

John's Gospel nourishes the soul and perplexes the mind. Called by Clement of Alexandria (ca. AD 188-210) the *spiritual* Gospel, its symbolism shines. Jesus is bread of life, light of the world, good shepherd, true vine, the way, the truth, and the life. John's Gospel "plays" on different octaves, attracting first readers and inspiring astute scholars who struggle to comprehend what is going on and why. A good commentary on John—and I hope mine joins that rank— must be able to play on several levels, appealing to soul and spirit, and mind as well.

For twelfth century Hildegard of Bingen *song* is metaphor for spiritual union with God. In a letter written during her eightieth year, she says:

> Therefore consider carefully that just as the body of Christ was born of the Holy Spirit from the integrity of the Virgin Mary, just so is the song of praise according to the heavenly music radiated by the Holy Spirit in the Church. The body is truly the garment of the soul, which has a living voice; for that reason it is fitting that the body simultaneously with the soul repeatedly sing praises to God through the voice. (Neuls-Bates: 19)

In meditations on the Prologue I include two early church hymns, which are indeed the heart's praise to God. Both were inspired by John's Prologue.

As you read and reflect upon the various portions of this book, I encourage you to combine your meditation with visual drama on that portion. Two rich resources are the DVD movie narrated by Christopher Plummer, *The Gospel of John*, based upon the *Today's English Version* (TEV), a translation by the American Bible Society: locate at (www.GospelofJohntheFilm.com) and the DVD by Jean Vanier on John's Gospel.

This book contains copious indexing of different genres: Nuggets (a brief recap of the John-chapter content), Drama (in some chapters), Meditation, Poetry, Song, and Art. These genres, however, cannot be discretely categorized: poetry, art, and song lyrics lead to "meditation." May all praise our living, loving Lord!

Spiritual Reflection

Thank you Jesus, for
the Bread you have given and now give us, and
the Bread you promise to give us.

Thank you Jesus, for
the Truth you have given and now give us, and
the Truth that you promise us through your Holy Spirit.

Thank you Jesus, for
the Life you have given and now give us, and
the Life you promise us eternally.

Praise be to the Father, the Son, and the Holy Spirit,
May your Triune name be magnified
through cross, resurrection, exaltation
lifted up so all might come and continue to believe
Jesus is the Christ;
Messiah is Jesus.

Jesus, thank you for this Gospel gift of light, life, and love!

Yours by grace upon grace, Willard

Prologue of John:
A song of invitation and grace
-Pamela Graf Short (with permission)

In the beginning was the Word
Word sings us an ancient song
of unrelenting love
of fresh hope
of painful rejection.
We are invited to join the song
we are invited
to receive
to believe
and to become children of God

In the beginning was the Word
 and the Word was with God...
With God in life
With God in light
With God in truth
With God in glory
With God in grace upon grace

All things came into being through Word
All things:
all persons, all planets, all stars,
all animals, all creatures of the sea
all grains of sand, all seeds, all tear drops,
all sounds
all the shades of blue
all the sources of thread—wool on the back of a lamb
and silk from a worm
and cotton from a thorny plant
and polyester from an oil can,
all came into being through *Word*

Without Word not one thing came into being
Not one thing can say it came on its own.
Not you or I
not a comedian or a chemist or a king

not John Calvin or Menno Simons or Martin Luther;
not Mother Teresa or Billy Graham
or even John the Baptist.
John the Baptist and all things
        stand as witnesses.
John the Baptist and all things join the song

The True Light which enlightens everyone
was coming into the world
True Light
Penetrating Light
Light shining through
my shame
my envy
my dullness
my shadows
my lost-ness
my shallowness
my fear
my ego
my distraction
my hostility
my pain

True Light
Penetrating Light
Light shining
into my center
into my goodness
into my capacities
to bring life
to speak truth
to communicate glory
to offer grace upon grace
to become children of God

Yet the world did not know Word...
Word's own people did not accept Word
Word was not received.
And thus the song becomes a moan

and the moan a whimper
and the whimper a wail
like a little babe left hungry and cold
the birth song of the humble One
the rejected One
the One who enters our pain

Yet to all who receive Word... Word
gives authority to become children of God

From Word's fullness we have all received
Grace upon Grace
Word does not stop calling us
Word does not stop believing in us
Word does not stop revealing
the Father's heart to us
full of grace upon grace
      upon grace upon grace
We are all invited
to receive,
to believe,
           and to become children of God.

John 1:1-18

John's Gospel Prologue

Nuggets

The *Word* occurs as stated subject only in vv. 1 and 14. The Word is the agent of creation, bringing *life* and *light* into the world (vv. 1-5). The darkness does not overcome the light. The Word becomes flesh, incarnate (v. 14), tenting among us with *glory, full of truth and grace. Jesus* as person is not named until 1:29.

The "only God-Son" *reveals* God (v. 18) and tells God's story in the Gospel.

John (the Baptist, though this descriptor never occurs in this Gospel) is *Witness* to the Word: witness to the Word as *light* of the world (vv. 6-9) and witness to *the Word made flesh* (vv. 15-17).

In the Prologue the *Word* bookends John the Witness, and John bookends the heart of the Prologue (vv. 9-14): *to all who received him, who believed in his name, he gave power to become the children of God* (v. 12) ...And the Word became flesh, and lived among us . . . (v. 14).

What is said of the *Word* is said of Wisdom (*Sophia*) in the OT. But this Gospel, whose author is anonymous from start to finish, never mentions *Wisdom*, one of the Gospel's numerous puzzles.

Meditation

1. Asserting all creation comes through the *Word* (the Prologue's *Logos*), Jacques Ellul affirms,
    Astronomers probe pulsars and quasars, speaking of billions of light-years, billions of degrees centigrade, billions of megawatts, and unimaginable explosions of energy. All this, encompassed in reality *within* the "God says," gives us an idea of the distance [and difference] between the Creator and us. These astronomic numbers represent merely the effect of a word, from God's point

7

of view. The word creates with supreme ease, so that in this sense word and action can be truly considered identical (54).

John's Gospel, beginning with creation, stretches the human mind beyond its limits. But then it touches us personally in the Word incarnate, in Jesus who thirsts, weeps, suffers, and dies.

2. Adrian van Kaam (89) offer words worth pondering:

> "As the divine Word of the Father, you are the expression of . . .[God's] fullness. You hold within you from all eternity all that exists and pre-exists in . . . [God's] caring, creative, and confirming love. We are, therefore, also held in you, his eternal Word."

3. Even though John, like Mark, has no Christmas birth stories, the Gospel does not lack motifs that are precious to Christian believers at Christmas time. In 2009, writing on the Prologue, I began our Christmas letter with these awesome, joyful lines from John:

> **Logos-Word** made *flesh*,
> We beheld his **Glory**
> **I AM** the **Light** of the world
> My *Peace* I give to you, not as the world gives
> So that your **Joy** may be full
> **Abide** in me, and I in you.
> I go to prepare a **Place** for you.

This is John's "Christmas" theology: *light* and *glory* pierce and dispel darkness, bringing *joy* and *peace*. John's Gospel gifts are *abiding-in-Jesus*, the true Vine (cup of covenant love unto death), the fruit of the God-Word become *flesh*, Jesus living and dying among us for our salvation (3:16; 6:51), and preparing an eternal home (*place*) for us (14:1-3).

4. In meditating on John 1 this brief phrase catches up the miraculous import of Jesus coming to dwell among us:

"God breaks into our time and space to hallow it."-Marlene Kropf, introducing Jesus' birth for worship (Belmont Mennonite Church, Jan. 2, 2011).

5. In her commentary on John's Prologue, Hildegard of Bingen (1098-1179) sees in her first vision a Trinitarian image—bearded head of God the Father, the winged figure of the Holy Spirit, carrying the Lamb (cf. John 1:29, 36), the Son—that echoes Israel's Wisdom tradition and speaks passionately of the creative power that John calls the *Word*:

I, the highest and fiery power,
have kindled every spark of life,
and I emit nothing that is deadly.
I decide on all reality.
With lofty wings I fly above the globe:
With wisdom I have rightly put the universe in order.
I, the fiery life of divine essence,
am aflame beyond the beauty of the meadows.
(Jasper: 71; Vision 1.2 in *Liber divinorum operum*, ca. 1173)

Song

1. John Michael Talbot's cantata, *Light Eternal*. The first piece in the
    musical, **"In The Beginning,"** connects to the heart. As you listen to
    it, you hear the lines in parentheses as under-voice to the dominant
    lines:

    > In the beginning (2x)
    > The Word was in God's presence
    >   (The Word was God)
    > in God's presence
    >   (The Word was God)
    > in God's presence
    >   (Through Him all things were made)
    > in the heavens
    >   (Through Him all things were made)
    > in the heavens
    > And the earth
    > Whatever came to be in Him
    > Found life
    > Life for the Light of man.
    >
    > The Word was light...
    > The Light shines in the darkness
    > The Word is Life
    > And God is the Life
    >
    > Whatever came to be in Him
    > Found life
    > Life for the Light of man.

    This lyric rightly perceives the Prologue doxologically, engaging the
    listener in worship. To appreciate fully the Prologue one must feel its
    doxological beauty and depth. [See the last entry for the
    Commentary's "Prologue": "The Text in the Life of the Church."]

2. An old hymn text by Aurelius Clemens Prudentius (AD 348–410;
    translated by John M. Neale and Henry W. Baker, 1851, 1861)
    expresses well the awesome mystery of creation from "Of the
    Father's love begotten" (stanzas 1 and 2):

10

Of the Father's love begotten, ere the worlds began to be,
he is Alpha and Omega, he the source, the ending he,
of the things that are and have been,
and that future years shall see,
evermore and evermore.

By his word was all created. He commanded and 'twas done.
Earth and sky and boundless oceans, universe of Three in One.
All that sees the moon's soft radiance,
and all that breathes beneath the sun,
Evermore and evermore. (*Hymnal: A Worship Book* 104)

The last two verses voice human and angelic praise for creation.

3. A still older text, "O joyous light of glory," with music that conveys the divine mystery, is attributed to the earlier church father, Athenogenes (2nd century), translated from the French by Mepkin Abbey, and likely translated earlier from the Greek. This is a good hymn for group study of the Gospel. The chant-music has irregular lengths of words and line-scores:

    Refrain
    O Joyous light of glory,
    eternal splendor of the Father,
    holy blessed Son, Jesus Christ.
    Stanzas
    1. Now as we come to the setting of the sun,
            the evening lamp is lit,
            We sing to the Father, the Son, and the Holy Spirit.

    2. At all times you are worthy to be praised with lips undefiled,
            O Son of God, Giver of Life,
            all creation sings your glory.

    3. Let my prayer, O Lord, arise before you like incense,
            and the raising of my hands
            be as an evening sacrifice.

    4. Therefore in celebrating your glory,
            we proclaim the love of the Father,
            in the light of the Spirit,
            burning seal which makes you one!
            (*Sing the Journey* 116)

4. A song lyric that catches up the marvelous glory of the Prologue is composed by former Gospel of John student, Adam Tice.

The glory of the living Son

(*Stanza 1*)
The glory of the living Son
    is touched, and seen, and heard—
In body and in spirit, one,
    the living, breathing Word.
He gave us life, he made the earth,
    but even in his might,
the Word was given human birth
    to be the world's true Light.

CMD Suggested tune, ELLACOMBE
©AML Tice, 2004 with GIA permission
For an AMBS chapel hymn-sing on John 1

Art

The distinctive art painting that appears here is from *The Saint John's Bible*, an enormous project inspired by Scripture and art. Since the time of Gutenberg's invention of the printing press (1452) the arduous, disciplined, careful task and gift of hand-written Scripture has been lost. This "art" began by writing on papyrus, then later on parchment made from calf-skin, and still later on paper. *The Saint John's Bible* project recreates that ancient skill. The monks through the ages embellished the text with art of many colors, often lavishly, especially for the first page of a biblical book. Among the most cherished from the medieval period are those in *The Treasures of Mount Athos: Illuminated Manuscripts* (Ekdotike Athenon S.A., Vol. 1, 1973; Vol. 2, 1982). These manuscripts were written in Greek. This 1970s publication of them is an art treasure of medieval text illuminations.

The Saint John's Bible is not a printing of work done centuries earlier, but a contemporary original production, with three of the projected seven volumes completed: *Pentateuch, Psalms, Gospels and Acts*. It is the fruit of disciplined devotion to sacred Scripture, rich both artistically and aesthetically. Indeed, in a time when book-making competes with electronic production of texts,

> *The Saint John's Bible* is a major artistic, cultural, and spiritual endeavor. It is the first handwritten and illuminated Bible commissioned since the invention of the printing press.
>
> Donald Jackson, world renowned calligrapher and illuminator, in collaboration with artists and theologians, has woven word and image in this once-in-a-millennium project.... The Word of God, hand-illuminated through ancient methods by a contemporary master, brings the reader to an epiphany of the sacred.... (*The Saint John's Bible* brochure).

In this spiritual endeavor text and image are twinned to enhance sacred Scripture as Word of God. The image is from *Gospels and Acts* (first page of John's Gospel) and appears also in Susan Sink's *THE ART OF THE SAINT JOHN'S BIBLE: A Reader's Guide to Pentateuch, Psalms, Gospels and Acts* (p. 91). The New Revised Standard Version (NRSV) is the text used for the beautiful, exquisite calligraphy of *The Saint John's Bible*.

Figure 1: Word Made Flesh

Word Made Flesh, Donald Jackson, Copyright 2002, *The Saint John's Bible*, Saint John's University, Collegeville, Minnesota USA.

John 1:19–2:12

A Week of New Creation

Nuggets

Why put the wedding in Cana (2:1-11) with Chapter 1? A recurring phrase, *the next day*, punctuates John 1 (vv. 29, 35, 43), for a total of four days. Add to this, *On the third day* of 2:1, and we get the title of this unit!

On the first day religious leaders from Jerusalem go out to question John: who are you? John depreciates his identity to only the *voice* of witness.

On the second day John hails the one whom he witnesses as *the Lamb of God who takes away the sin of the world* (v.29) and recounts Jesus' baptism.

On the third day we meet *Jesus* (first time in the Gospel) to whom John transfers *two of his disciples: Andrew and one forever unnamed!*

Note these first words:

-Jesus: *"what are you looking for?"*

-the two disciples: *"where are you staying"* (the verb *abide* in John 15).

-Jesus' response, *"Come and see"* (1:39)

Andrew finds his brother, Simon. Jesus changes his name to Peter.

On the fourth day Jesus goes to Galilee and finds Philip, and calls him, *"Follow me"* (the only disciple thus called in this Gospel, until 21:19 when Peter hears the same)! Philip finds Nathaniel, a character not in Matthew, Mark, and Luke. Nathaniel, one without deceit, contra Jacob his pillow predecessor, *"will see heaven opened and the angels of God ascending and descending upon the Son of Man."* Mystery surrounding *Son of Man* begins.

Three days later, they go to a wedding at Cana. Jesus' mother—*woman on Jesus' lips* (as in 4:21 and 20:15 this vocative signals Jesus' momentous self-revelation about to occur)—takes charge and has full confidence in her son's wedding qualifications. Not until 3:29 do we learn who the bridegroom is, at the symbolic level of reading John. Wine, the sign of the new age, at a *wedding* opens the door to the Gospel's announcing the new age come with joy and celebration! This is Jesus' first *sign*; many glorify God.

Spiritual Reflection

Logos

        Creating Life

                Generating Light

                        Driving back the darkness

                                Lamb, taking away the world's sin

Wedding

        renewing covenant

Bridegroom

        making wine for the betrothed

                                  Willard

Meditation

1. In his DVD on John, Jean Vanier says Jesus' first words, *"What are you looking for?"* (1:38) are central to human desire. Vanier's answer is that desire for friendship, closeness to another person, is at the heart of human desire. Later in John, Jesus tells his disciples, "I do not call you servants any longer, ...but I have called you friends" (15:15). What drew you into and keeps you in a church body? Many people value friendships, a vital part of knowing and growing in Jesus. What are you looking for?
2. Learning to pray, personally and corporately, aids faith formation. The two Anabaptist Prayer books (see Boers, ed., in the Bibliography) contribute richly to that process. Spiritual friendships or spiritual direction contribute to ongoing formation into the image of Christ (2 Cor 3:17-18). Ask yourself: in what way does disciple-commitment aid formation into Christ's image?
3. The two patterns of teachers finding disciples in the Greco-Roman world occur in this Gospel: the summons and response for Philip *only*, and the coming to or gathering around a teacher through the testimony of another, the dominant model in John. Jesus is teacher; disciples are learners seeking to understand Jesus' teaching and be formed as his faithful disciples. Jesus' response to the disciples' inquiry, "Where do you live?" is "Come and see" (1:39, 46).

Song

1. Sing "Come and see" (*Hymnal: A Worship Book* 20) and "Listen, God is calling" (*Sing the Journey* 42). How do you respond to the third meditation and these songs?

2. Talbot's *Light Eternal* combines the image of *Lamb of God who takes away the sins of the world* with *bread of life* (John 6). Listen to this rendition and read Psalm 51:7-10.

3. The range of music related to this section embraces Samuel Barber's *Agnus Dei* as well as Johnny Cash's "He turned the water into wine." Find their texts on the internet.

John 2:13–4:3

From Old to New: Temple, Birth, Baptism

Communities in Conflict

Nuggets

This unit begins with a time-marker: *The Passover of the Jews was near.* It also shifts location, from Galilee/Cana to *Jerusalem.* The dramatic event is Jesus' cleansing the temple. In John, Jesus' temple-cleansing begins Jesus' *Jerusalem* ministry. Jesus' temple demonstration raises hackles for the religious leaders— and questions for the reader. Was Jesus violent? *No,* his *whip of cords* was used on *the sheep and the cattle* (2:15). Jesus says, *destroy this temple and in three days I will raise it up* (v. 20).

Temple, like *born again/anew* or *from above* in Jesus' words to Nicodemus, has double meaning causing misunderstanding— a recurring literary feature of the Gospel. The Jewish temple, institutions, feasts, and rituals must be transformed to serve all humanity; they must be no longer location-specific.

Nicodemus comes to Jesus at night to inquire about entering the kingdom of God. He hears he must undergo rebirth for the new order. Does the water of rebirth (echo baptism) complement the wine of the wedding, so that these events are intimations of baptism and Lord's Supper? Only John 3:3, 5 speaks of *the kingdom of God* (cf. 18:36), a dominant theme in the Synoptics. John speaks often of *eternal life,* with present and future impact.

John 3:16 sums up John's evangelistic challenge (cf. 3:36). Jesus comes to save the world, not condemn it (3:17). The polarities of light and darkness, belief or unbelief, emerge in Jesus' dialogue with Nicodemus (vv. 2-12) and the following discourse.

The end of John 3 and 4:1-3 sharply clarifies the relation between John and Jesus on purification and baptism. Again John is Witness to Jesus, and now also comes a surprise: he is the *friend of the bridegroom* (3:29). Recall the wedding; who is the bridegroom?

Celebrate wedding *joy*, a gem, to reappear symbolically in Samaria!

Call to Worship

L. We come together as the church of Jesus Christ,
 recognizing that our Lord lived and died,
 not just for the church, but for all people,
 God's highest creation.

L. For God so loved the world that he gave his only Son.

P. We also recognize that in God's great love,
 we sense our need first to be loved
 and thus to be turned around,
 to face the needs of others.

L. We love, because God first loved us.

P. Let us love, then, so that we may be free of selfish desires,
 Liberated to strive for God's will.

L. Whatever we do to the least of God's family,
 that we do to our Lord.

Willard E. Roth (adapted), in *Words of Worship*, 112.
Edited by Arlene Mark;
Based on John 3:16; 1 John 4:19; Matt. 6:33; 12:50; 25:40.

22

Drama Dialogue

Consider this Skit for presentation to your congregation
(presented at Belmont Mennonite Church, Spring 2011)

Born From Above
Written by Jen Helmuth Shenk, based on John 3:1-17 (with permission)
Characters: Jesus, Nicodemus

Jesus is sitting by a fire, pantomiming warming his hands as he rests. Nicodemus enters from the side, looking cautiously over his shoulder, as if he is being followed. He is somewhat skittish, but is determined to talk to Jesus in order to satisfy his nagging questions (as you'll see, he has a lot of them!).

N: Excuse me, Rabbi?

J: Yes? What brings you here at this late hour?

N: I'm Nicodemus, a member of the Jewish ruling council, and I hope you know we have deep respect for your teachings?

J: Yes, I know who you are.

N: Well, we all know you're a teacher straight from God. All your miracles and signs point right to God, so there's no way you could make all this happen unless God were in on it, right?

J: You're absolutely right. Take it from me: Unless a person is **born from above**, it's not possible to see the Kingdom of God.

N: **Born from above?** (*pausing in confusion*) How can anyone be born who has already *been born* and *grown up*? You can't re-enter your mother's womb and be born again. What are you talking about?

J: You're not listening. Let me say it again. No one can enter the Kingdom of God unless they submit to being born in the Spirit. Made new. (*Pointing to Nicodemus' body*) Flesh gives birth to flesh, but Spirit (*pointing above*) gives birth to spirit. You know what I'm talking about... the invisible moving the visible. The person deep inside your shell of a body—your complete essence of who you were created to be. THAT must be made new by God's Spirit and given new life.

N: *(gives a blank look)* New life?

J: *(patiently continuing, but increasing in passion)* Don't be surprised when I tell you that you have to be **'born from above.'** I'll put it to you in plain terms. You know what the wind is like, right? You can hear it rustling through the trees. You can see it blowing the branches this way and that. But you have no idea where it's coming from, or where it's headed next. *That's* the way it is with everyone who is **'born from above'** by the Spirit of God—the wind of God.

N: What do you mean by this? How does this happen? How did we get from being born to talking about winds blowing?

J: You say you're a member of the Jewish council. A brilliant, respected *teacher* of Israel.

N: *(not realizing the irony, standing taller with pride)* Yes, a prominent one. I studied for many years at the temple. Why?

J: By the way, if this Jewish Council thing doesn't end up working out, you should consider trying out for Jeopardy since you're so good at asking questions.

N: Jeopardy? What is Jeopardy?

J: Never mind. Now, Listen carefully. I know what you're doing. Instead of facing the evidence of what you've seen with your own eyes, and heard with your own ears, you're taking the coward's way out. You're procrastinating, putting off taking this step of faith by asking question after question.

N: *(frustrated, defensive)* Is it wrong to want to understand? To have it make sense in my mind? Do you realize what you're saying isn't even logical?

J: If I'm telling you about earthly things that you can see as plainly as the hand before your face, and you don't believe me, what's the use of trying to talk about things you *can't* see? No one has gone into the presence of God except (*gesturing to himself*) the Son of Man. In all your studies, you've read how Moses lifted up the serpent in the desert, giving people something concrete to see so they could believe. It's the same way with the (*gesturing to himself*) Son of Man—who was sent by God to be lifted up so everyone who looks up to him, trusting and expectant, will gain real life: Eternal life.

N: (*in wonder, slowly*) Eternal life?

J: (*passionately and tenderly*) For God so loved the world that he gave his one and only Son, that whoever believes in him will not perish, but have eternal life. God didn't send his Son into the world just to point an accusing finger, telling the world how horrible it was. He came to help. To put things right again.

N: You've given me much to think about, Rabbi. You'll understand if I need more time to ponder this idea of being **born from above**? (*beginning to exit*)

J: (*shakes his head and sighs, going back to warming his hands over the fire, humming the Jeopardy theme song...*)

Meditation

1. My last entry in "The Text in the Life of the Church" (*John*, BCBC Commentary) emphasizes the evangelistic appeal of John 3:16. For a philosophical analysis of the text that stimulates our cognitive curiosity, please check:
http://www.heraldpress.com/bcbc/john.
The beloved hymn "For God so loved us" ("Gott ist die Liebe," *Hymnal: A Worship Book* 167) catches up both dimensions. Meditate on the lyrics of the hymn in tandem with the diagrams in the Commentary and the Website.

2. Talbot's **Eternal Light** in *Light Eternal* emphasizes needing and receiving God's light and love to pierce our darkness. It's striking that this theme (3:18-21) follows the Nicodemus-Jesus "at night" encounter. Listen!

Art
Figure 2. Nicodemus
What impressions does this night-time scene stir in you?

Artist: Henry O. Tanner,
Title: Nicodemus   Date:1899.
Description: Oil on canvas. Size: 33 11/16 x 39 ½ in. (85.6 x 100.3 cm).
Acc. No.: 1900.1.
Courtesy of the Pennsylvania Academy of Fine Arts, Philadelphia.
Joseph E. Temple Fund.

Introduction to the "Transformation" Art Image

In 2011 the Belmont Mennonite Church's Worship Commission requested one of our members, artist Kris A. Shenk, to create an art piece appropriate for the Advent preparation for newness of life. One morning the "gift" took shape in her art-imagination. She asked people to bring their "stuff" (things not used and about to be disposed) and then, trusting the Spirit to guide, she began her work. The first Sunday the curving green lines soaring heavenward appeared (a disposed garden hose). Each Sunday more and more of the "stuff" (for example, *Readers Digest* covers for the lower right fan-like semi-circle) added to the transforming invitation, expressed well by the hymn, "Beauty for Brokenness" (*Sing the Story* 115; listen to the CD, *Sing the Story 2*, conducted by Kenneth Nafziger and performed by the Story Musicians, to hear this lovely song).

Art speaks to people in different ways. As our Sunday school class discussed this marvelous gift of art to our congregational worship, it was clear that Kris and many others saw "transformation" in this piece—the worn stuff of life transformed into beauty evoking worship, lifting us heavenward.

John's Gospel doesn't use the word "transformed," though Paul's writings do. Putting this into John's symbolic world, I thought of *anōthen*, Jesus' call to Nicodemus. It means "born from above, born anew or born again." That which was "from below" had become that which orients us now to that "from above." We are tugged heavenward by an artist's trust that something good and beautiful could emerge from discarded stuff.

Sing and pray the chorus, "Wind, wind, blow on me, wind, wind set me free" and conclude with, "blessed Holy Spirit," the power-source for transformation that John 3 invites us to receive.

God, give us faith to believe, that what we do and use in ordinary life can by your gift of new life link us to your divine being and beauty, to your love for each of us.

Figure 3: "Transformation"/ *Anōthen* (John's Gospel)

Mosaic by Kris A. Shenk
Description: 48" x 96" on a sheet of plywood with "mixed media
materials" (used with non-exclusive permission).
Courtesy of Jen Shenk Photography

My own new verse for the "Beauty for Brokenness" hymn, inspired by this art is:

> Beauty from stuff disposed, transformed anew.
> Spirit creating, life from above.
> Gift from the artist's hand, for all who see,
> Hope from God rising, Spirit renewed.
> Take all our stuff, birth it anew,
> Fill us with hope, love and peace,
> Smelt all the old, form it for Christ,
> Transform our stuff into joyous life.

John 4:4-54

Jesus' Peace-Mission into Samaria

Savior of the World

Nuggets

The location shifts again, now from Jerusalem to Samaria for the greater part of the unit, but also to Galilee, for the second story, where again in Cana Jesus does his second sign. Jesus has a new dialogue partner: the Samaritan woman, quite a contrast to Nicodemus—likely arranged by the author to accentuate the contrasting responses.

The central motifs are: Jesus gives living water and lifts worship above *place* (Gerizim or Jerusalem) to *manner*: in spirit and truth.

Jesus' *must* (4:4) mission into Samaria is a Gospel gem. His dialogue with the Samaritan woman stuns: from living water to husbands to worship. At a figural level the sequence of topics is a seamless whole (see Commentary).

The woman perceives Jesus first as a Jew (*strange*, to be in Samaria), then prophet, and then possibly the Messiah, because he transcends *place* of worship with *manner* of worship. Jesus then shocks her (the narrative plot and us) by disclosing himself as *I AM* (4:26; cf. Exod 3:13-15).

The woman leaves; Jesus' disciples return (27). The woman testifies to her home-folk (28-29). Jesus speaks to and commissions his disciples into the Samaritan (!) fields *ripe for harvest* (31-38)! *Many Samaritans believed in him because of the woman's testimony* (v. 39). They invite Jesus to come and he stays two days and many more believe. They exclaim: *truly [you are] the Savior of the world* (42).

The encounter breaks racial, ritual, cultural, and national boundaries; it's truly a peace-making mission. Jesus then goes to Galilee and heals a Roman official's son without going to his house, but only saying, *"Go, your son will live"* (vv. 46-52). It *happens* as he speaks. This second *sign* in Cana also breaks barriers of enmity: a Jew heals a Gentile!

Drama Dialogue (by Author, wms)

A man and a woman reenact Jesus' conversation with the woman of Samaria. At first, the woman responds with superior tone and touch of sarcasm, but this then shifts to surprise and awe.

She came to draw water

Jesus says to her   *Samaritan woman says to him*

"Give me a drink."

                                                       "How is it that you, a Jew, ask a
                                                       drink of me, a woman of
                                                       Samaria?"

"If you knew the gift of God,
and who it is that is saying to you,
'Give me a drink,' you would have asked him,
and he would have given you living water."

                                                       "Sir, you have no bucket, and
                                                       the well is deep.
                                                       Where do you get that living
                                                       water?
                                                       Are you greater than our
                                                       ancestor Jacob,who gave us the
                                                       well, and with his sons and his
                                                       flocks drank from it?"

"Everyone who drinks of this water
will be thirsty again,
but those who drink of the water
that I will give them will never be thirsty.
The water that I will give will become
in them a spring of water gushing up
         to eternal life."

                                                       "Sir, give me this water, so that
                                                       I may never be thirsty or have to
                                                       keep coming here to draw
                                                       water."

"Go, call your husband, and come back."

                                                       "I have no husband."

"You are right in saying, 'I have no husband';
for you have had five husbands,
and the one you have now is not your husband.
What you have said is true!"

"Sir, I see that you are a
prophet.
Our ancestors
worshiped on this
mountain, but you say
that the place where
people must worship is
in Jerusalem."

"Woman, believe me, the hour is coming
        when you will worship the Father
neither on this mountain nor in Jerusalem.
You worship what you do not know;
        we worship what we know,
        for salvation is from the Jews.
But the hour is coming, and is now here,
when the true worshipers will worship the
Father in spirit and truth, for the Father
seeks such as these to worship him.
God is spirit, and those who worship him
        must worship in spirit and truth."

"I know that Messiah is
coming" (who is called
Christ). "When he
comes, he will proclaim
all things to us."

"I am he, the one who is speaking to you."

Poetry
Reflection

God of Spirit and Fire
Who baptizes us with living water
Immerse us in your love
That we may gain belief for the journey ahead.
In the name of Jesus. Amen

God of relationship
Whose presence draws people together
Open my hands
So that I may enter your story of visionary restoration
In the name of the Wounded One. Amen

God of spirit and truth
Who encounters humans in the physical act of drinking water
Break into our hungry world
So that the love you offer will move us
       beyond our borders to bring healing and hope to the world.
In the name of The Reconciling One. Amen

Confronting God
Whose truth moves into the wells of our hearts
Open up the way for us
That in seeking your face we will encounter our sisters and brothers.
In the name of Jesus. Amen.

Lois Siemens, AMBS student, 2004 (used with permission)

Song: A traveler unknown to me

A traveler unknown to me
        was waiting when I reached the well.
He asked me gently for a drink,
        but I asked why he couldn't tell
that I was not the same as he.
Why would this stranger speak to me?

He said, "If you knew who I am
        and if you knew what God has done,
you would have asked for, and received,
        life-giving water, thirsty one."
He told me all I've ever done;
the past from which I try to run.

He smiled, and said, "If you will drink,
        You'll never thirst but ever live!
Eternal life wells up within-
        this is the water that I give."
Much more than prophet, more than lord:
        is this the Christ, the living word?

"I am the one of whom you speak!
        I see you trust what you have heard.
If you would share the love I bring,
        then go, a preacher of the Word!"
What mystery, that Christ would show
        this Love through me, for all to know.

What mystery, the awesome love
        the Traveler Unknown has taught.
Among rejected people, found
        true worshippers the Spirit sought.
What mystery, that love unbound
In truth and spirit can be found.

Adam Tice, AMBS student, 2006 (with GIA permission)
88.88.88 Suggested tune: VERNON
©2003, AML Tice. Full text in *Singing the New Testament*, The Calvin Institute of Christian Worship and Faith Alive Christian Resources, 2008, set to SUSSEX CAROL

> This ballad is based upon Charles Wesley's "Wrestling Jacob." Both stories involve people struggling with their own identity and the identity of God. A further connection is that Jesus met the Samaritan woman at Jacob's well.

Art

Janeth Norfleete Day devotes much of her book to "As Artists Have Painted Her" (43-120), followed with English-speaking writers' depiction of the woman of Samaria in literature (121-45). This image below makes us rethink stereotypical images regarding the Samaritan woman's cultural status and morality. In the Eastern Church (twelfth century) she is highly honored and named Saint Photeine (see "The Text in the Life of the Church" in my BCBC *John* Commentary on John 4). This image appears on several websites, among them, that of the Saint Takla Haymanout Coptic Orthodox Church-Alexandria, Egypt.

Figure 4. Jesus and the Samaritan Woman

Also at: http://praying.kansasbob.com/2010_12_01_archive.html
(copyright source and artist unknown).

John 5

Jesus Works God's Work

"Trial" Begins

Nuggets

The location shifts again, back to Jerusalem. Jesus does his third sign, healing a lame man at the large purification pool of Bethzatha on the Sabbath. Jesus then begins intense debate with opponents.The Jews, presumably religious leaders and certainly not all Jews, begin persecuting Jesus (v. 16).

Jesus defends himself, saying, *"My Father is still working, and I also am working"* (v. 17). The Jews accuse him of making himself *equal to God*. Jesus justifies his working on the Sabbath because he is doing his Father's work, an offense that is blasphemous. Is Jesus equal to God?

Is there irony here? The accusing Jews speak what the believing reader knows in a sense the Jews here do not know (see Commentary)?

Jesus takes the defense and then prosecutes his accusers. He identifies witnesses to himself, which the accusing Jews, while accepting in principle, deny in practice because they refuse to believe in him to whom Scripture points (vv. 38-40). Their failure lies in seeking human glory rather than God's (vv. 41, 44). Jesus defers judgment of them but says, Moses accuses you before the Father, the One and final Judge.

Meditation

1. Jesus' healing of the lame man by the pool raises numerous questions about divine healing and its relation to modern medicine, with its competence to heal as well. Sirach, a Wisdom book regarded as Scripture by the Roman Catholic, Orthodox, and early Anabaptist church traditions, contains an early text (ca. 200 BCE) that links the two:

    Honor physicians for their services, for the Lord created them;
      for their gift of healing comes from the Most High...
    The skill of physicians makes them distinguished, and in the
      presence of the great they are admired.

> The Lord created medicines out of the earth, and the sensible will not despise them...[the Lord] gave skill to human beings that he might be glorified in his marvelous works. By them [the medicines] the physician heals and takes away pain; the pharmacist makes a mixture from them. God's works will never be finished; and from him health spreads over all the earth.
>
> My child, when you are ill, do not delay, but pray to the Lord, and he will heal you. Give up your faults and direct your hands rightly, and cleanse your heart from all sin...
>
> Then give the physician his place, for the Lord created him; do not let him leave you, for you need him.There may come a time when recovery lies in the hands of physicians, for they too pray to the Lord that he grant them success in diagnosis and in healing, for the sake of preserving life. He who sins against his Maker, will be defiant toward the physician. (Sir 38:1-15)

How do you understand the relation between God and modern medicine for healing? For extensive treatment of biblical teaching on healing and health care, see Swartley, *Health, Healing, and the Church's Mission: Biblical Perspectives and Moral Priorities* (InterVarsity Press, 2012).

2. Look in the "Praising/Adoring" section of *Hymnal: A Worship Book*, 106-127 (or one with which you are most familiar) and notice how these hymns are addressed to God, Jesus, Holy Spirit. Sometimes "Lord" is addressed, which may mean either God or Christ. In your worship, do you freely adore the Triune God, or wonder about worship of Jesus directly or the Holy Spirit? John's Gospel points us to the oneness and unity of the Godhead.

3. John 5 raises the relationship of Jesus to God (v. 18). Meditate on the five stanzas of "At the name of Jesus" (*Hymnal: A Worship Book* 342). This hymn recognizes the distinction between the Son and the Father and also their shared divine identity. How do you understand the relation between the Father, the Son, and the Holy Spirit? Sing the worship chorus: "Father, we adore you." Then repeat with "Jesus" and "Spirit."

John 6

Jesus: I am the Bread of Life

Nuggets

The location shifts, back to Galilee. It's Passover time again, early spring. This is the second Passover. Recall the first in 2:13.

John 6 narrates *signs* four (Feeding the 5000) and five (Walking on Water). Jesus' discourse, taking off from the bread-sign revolves around his promise to satisfy spiritual hungers now and *raise... up on the last day*.

The miracle of the feeding introduces Jesus' extended discourse on *I am the bread of life*. But before this *I am* claim Jesus reveals himself *walking on the water* as the truly awesome *I AM*, echoing God's special identity-disclosure to Moses in Exodus 3:13-15.

Since John does not have any "institution" of the Lord's Supper, many regard John 6 as Eucharistic: Jesus commands his followers to *eat my flesh and drink my blood* (vv. 53-56). Understanding these words is difficult, but Jesus' gift of *eternal life, raised up on the last day*, promises hope that goes beyond understanding (cf. Phil 4:7).

In 6:66 many of Jesus' *disciples turned back and no longer went with him*, but Peter and the twelve pledge loyalty to Jesus. Peter confesses, "*We have come to believe and know that you are the Holy One of God.*" Jesus then introduces a somber pronouncement: one of you will defect. Satan has already entered into Judas. But this sadness cannot nullify Jesus' unfathomable gift: *the bread that I will give for the life of the world is my flesh* (v. 51).

Meditation

Though John's Gospel has no institution of the Lord's Supper, many commentators believe John 6 is Eucharistic. Two complementary pieces for meditation come from Anabaptist Balthasar Hubmaier and from Roman Catholic Jean Vanier.

1. In preparing for the Lord's Supper, Hubmaier writes:

Let a person test himself, whether he has a proper inward and fervent hunger for the bread which comes down from heaven, from which one truly lives, and thirst for the drink which flows into eternal life, to eat and drink both in the spirit, faith, and truth, as Christ teaches us in John 4; 6; and 7. If the spiritual eating and drinking does not first take place, then the outward breaking of bread, eating and drinking is a killing letter, 2 Cor 3:6; 1 Cor 11:29, hypocrisy, and the kind of food and drink whereby one eats condemnation and drinks death, as Adam did with the forbidden fruit of the tree in Paradise, Gen 3:6. (Hubmaier: 396-97)

2. In his spiritual probing of John's Gospel, Vanier writes on John 6 (the "separation" in the first line evokes OT sacrificial practice, where the blood was drained and the covenant people ate the flesh/meat of the sacrifice):

When Jesus uses the separation of flesh and blood,
he is signifying his death; he has come as the Lamb of God
who will be sacrificed and eaten as the Paschal Lamb.
Jesus is offering to us a personal, intimate relationship with him
that will lead us into the very life of God and nourish this life.
It will bring us to dwell in Jesus and to have Jesus dwell in us.

To let Jesus dwell in us means that we have cleaned up
the house of our hearts
in order to give him space so that he can live in us.
We are no longer filled up with ourselves.
We find our joy now in being and living with Jesus, the Beloved,
and in doing what he asks of us.
(Vanier: 126-27)

Song

1. John Michael Talbot's musical, *Light Eternal*, with its captivating soprano and tenor duet on "I am the Bread of Life," lifts us above contentious discussions of "eating my flesh" and "drinking my blood" to feasting on Jesus as life, peace, and healing.
Lines in parentheses overlap with and extend the dominant lines (used with permission):

> I am the Bread of Life
>   (Take this bread)
> I am meek and lowly of heart
>   (It is my body broken for you)
> I am the Living Water
>   (Take this cup drink from this cup)
> I am poured out for
>   (It is my blood shed for you)
> The life of the world.
>
> I am the Lamb of God
>   (Lamb of God love of God)
> The Chosen One
>   (Who takes away)
> To forgive the sins of the world
>   (This world's sin)
> I am the Light of God
>   (Lamb of God Light of God)
> To guide our feet
>   (Grant to us)
> To the way of peace
>   (Grant us peace)
>
> Lord, Lord we are not
>   (Lord, Lord)
> Worthy to receive you
> Lord, Lord only speak your word
>   (Lord, Lord)
> Only speak your word
> And we shall be healed
> We shall be healed.

2. Meditate on the wonderful hymn, "I am the Bread of Life," with its refrain "And I will raise you up" (*Hymnal: A Worship Book* 472), by Sarah Toolan. Jesus' promise in the refrain strengthens faith and hope:

Refrain
And I will raise you up (3x)
on the last day.

I am the bread of life.
You who come to me shall not hunger,
and who believe in me shall not thirst.
No one can come to me
unless the Father beckons.

> The bread that I will give
> is my flesh for the life of the world,
> and if you eat of this bread,
> you shall live forever (2x).

> I am the resurrection,
> I am the life.
> If you believe in me,
> even though you die,
> you shall live forever.

> Yes, Lord, I believe
> that you are the Christ,
> the Son of God,
> who has come
> into the world.

3. Another hymn, expressing gratitude for Jesus' broken body, is "Bread of Life" (*Hymnal: A Worship Book* 455). Its text by Kenneth I. Morse and music by Wilbur E. Brumbaugh are rich.

Bread of life, whose body, broken,
feeds the hunger of my heart,
may the thanks that you have spoken
bless each loaf I break apart.

Let these hands now calmly folding
speak my gratitude for grace,
lest the treasure I am holding
disappear before my face.

Lord, I welcome you to table;
grace my supper ever new.
With your feast of love enable
ev'ry guest to live for you.

Spiritual Reflection

Jesus as Bread of Life

You, Jesus, speak often of yourself as bread,
bread of life

bread that comes down from heaven,
from "my Father who gives you
the true bread from heaven" (v. 33)

"I am the bread of life" (v. 35)

And the Jews murmured, because you said,
"I am the bread that came down from heaven" (v. 41)

I am the bread of life (v. 48)

You said again
"This is the bread that comes down from heaven,
so that one may eat of it and not die" (v. 50)

"I am the living bread that came down from heaven,
Whoever eats of this bread will live forever;
and the bread that I will give
for the life of the world
is my flesh" (v. 51)

Jesus, on this bread may I munch always, Willard

John 7

Jesus: Living Water

The Feast of Tabernacles

Nuggets

The location continues, first, in Galilee, but then shifts to Jerusalem. The occasion for the journey is the Feast of Booths (Tabernacles). This celebration is marked by much *water-*pouring during the day and dancing under *lights* at night. It is a feast of rejoicing, and the key symbol is living water (v. 38).

Jesus delays going up to Jerusalem with his brothers because his *hour had not yet come*. But then he goes up anyway and holds forth twice: at the middle of the seven-day Festival (17-24), with response-repercussions.

Pharisees send police to arrest Jesus (v. 32). They hear his last, great day of the Festival's speech (37-39). Stunned by his words, the police return empty-handed (45-46).

The authorities fear Jesus' popularity, and belittle the police, who say of Jesus, *"Never has anyone spoken like this."* Nicodemus prevents the Council's plot: he must be tried before he can be judged (v. 50).

The Pharisees, saving face, grumble, saying, *no prophet is to arise from Galilee*. They demean Galilee (v. 52). Opposition between Galilee (safety) and Jerusalem (danger) appears.

The heart of the chapter hinges on the significance of the Feast of Booths, and Jesus' relationship to it. Jesus claims for himself fulfillment of the festival's significance. He (and his believers) is (are) the source of living water (7:37-39).

Meditation

Jean Vanier connects John 7:37 to Matthew 11:28:

> Only those who are heavy burdened and thirsty
> will discover the immensity of the love of Jesus
> and his desire to comfort and fulfill us.
>
> To drink from Jesus is to receive new life through his presence of
> love and enter into a personal relationship of trust with him.
> We "drink" his words,
> which cut through the chains of despair that imprison us.
> Jesus reveals to us then who we *are*
> and who we are called to *become*.
> We are loved by God, beloved of God.
> We, too, will do beautiful things;
> We, too, can give life to others.
> (Vanier: 137)

Song

1. Sing the hymn-text of Jesus' invitation, "O let all who thirst"
   (*Hymnal: A Worship Book* 495):

   O let all who thirst, let them come to the water. (let them come)
   And let all who have nothing,
   let them come to the Lord: (to the Lord)
   without money, without price. Why should you pay the price,
   except for the Lord? (for the Lord?)

   And let all who seek, let them come to the water. (let them come)
   And let all who have nothing,
   let them come to the Lord: (to the Lord)
   without money, without strife. Why should you spend your life,
   except for the Lord? (for the Lord?)

   And let all who toil, let them come to the water. (let them come)
   And let all who are weary,
   let them come to the Lord: (to the Lord)
   all who labor without rest. How can your soul find rest,
   except for the Lord? (for the Lord?)

And let all the poor, let them come to the water. (let them come)
Bring the ones who are laden,
bring them all to the Lord: (to the Lord)
Bring the children without might. Easy the load and light:
come to the Lord. (to the Lord)

2. Another "heart" hymn is "Jesus, Rock of ages," *Hymnal: A Worship Book* 515. Sing and repeat it until the Spirit (John 7:39) births life and true worship within you:

Jesus, Rock of ages, let me hide myself in thee.
Jesus, living Water, let me drink from your flowing stream.

3. Musical contribution by AMBS student, Adam Tice

I AM the Living Water
Swartley 13.13.13.13.13.13

I AM the living water that cools your thirsting soul.
I AM the bread of heaven that makes your living full.
I AM the Light to guide you I give you heaven's sight.
I AM the gentle shepherd that guards you in the night.
I AM the Vine in season, my wine will fill your cup.
I AM the Resurrection and I will raise you up.

Spiritual Reflection

I am grateful for the Holy Spirit
    rivers of water flowing out
        from Jesus and through believers.
           Thank you, Jesus,
                Giver of the Spirit.
Water
    Cleansing
        Flowing
           Blessing
                Healing (Rev 22)
    Jesus is the Source of the Water
        fulfilling the daily libations
           cleansing as Lamb of God.
        Water in the desert (Isa 43-44)
           quenching my soul's thirst.
Bread of Life
    You, Jesus, give yourself as
        Bread and drink for me
    so I must eat and drink
    continuing to chew on the bread
        and savoring the drink
    life-giving power for our
        own fleshy, vulnerable life in this world.
Light of the world
    I come, I come
        To You, to You
    The Light for all people
    Dispel the darkness
        so I can see
    Bind and loose the evil
        so I am free
The Son sets me free
        and I am free indeed.
    Touch my eyes
        with your healing light
So I see all things clearly.
        Thank you, Jesus   Willard

John 8

Truth on Trial

Jesus and the Pharisees—"The Jews"

Nuggets

The location of Jerusalem and the occasion of the Feast of Tabernacles continue from chapter 7. Jesus' claim, "I am the light of the world" together with this gem, *"If you continue in my word, you are truly my disciples; and you will know the truth, and the truth will make you free,"* leads to sharp controversy.

An intra-Jewish argument (Jesus and the accusing Jews) develops bitterly, hinging on the key word, Father, and this question: who is Jesus' Father and who is the father of the Jews who oppose Jesus? This argument does not provide a moral exemplar for us in our differences within the church(es).

I have chosen for our meditation and spiritual formation the parts of this chapter that function positively for us.

Meditation

John 8 presents a sharp call to walk in the light to escape the darkness of unbelief. How do we assure ourselves that we are not walking in darkness, but in the light of day? First, believe the claims Jesus made about himself, and practice John's love ethic. Second, meditate on light imagery. In the NT baptism was understood as "putting on the garment of light." Early Church Fathers understood baptism as putting off evil and putting on the garment of light (de Waal: 82-84, 110). In his transfiguration Jesus is encircled with light.This provides a model for the baptismal tradition of being clothed with light as we begin our new walk in the light (1 John 1:6-8). In Paul *light* comes by conversion, baptism, and new life (2 Cor 4:3-6; Eph 4:24; 5:8, 14-15). Thus, "…lay aside the works of darkness and put on the armor of light" (Rom 13:12).

Song

1. "Longing for light" (*Sing the Journey* 54)
    orients our spirit to the light:
    Refrain
    Christ, be our light! Shine in our hearts.
    Shine through the darkness.
    Christ, be our light!
    Shine in your church gathered today.

    Stanzas 1 and 3
    Longing for light, we wait in darkness.
    Longing for truth, we turn to you.
    Make us your own, your holy people,
    light for the world to see.

    Longing for food, many are hungry.
    Longing for water, many still thirst.
    Make us your bread, broken for others,
    shared until all are fed.

    > Tune: "Christ, be our light"
    > "Longing for Light"(c) 1993, Bernadette Farrel and
    > OCP, 5536 NE Hassalo, Portland, OR 97213.
    > All rights reserved. Used with permission.

2. Another plea for Christ to be our/my light occurs at the
    beginning and end of the prayer-hymn, "Jesus, be the center"
    (*Sing the Story* 31). Both stanzas 1 and 4 implore Jesus to "be
    my light."

3. A Christmas song, "Jesus, the Light of the World," arranged by George D. Elderkin (1890) beautifully links John's Prologue to chapter 8 on the *light* motif. "A "sixteenth *rest*" before each sixteenth note, gives it a life-giving beat and lilt toward light.

    Hark! The herald angels sing—Jesus; the Light of the world.
    Glory to the new born King, Jesus the Light, of the world.

    Joyful all ye nations rise—Jesus; the Light of the world.
    Join the triumph of the skies, Jesus the Light, of the world.

    Christ by highest heaven adored—Jesus; the Light of the world
    Christ, the everlasting Lord, Jesus the Light, of the world.

    Hail! the heav'n-born Prince of peace—Jesus; the Light of the world
    Hail! the son of righteousness, Jesus, the Light, of the world.

    Refrain
    We'll walk in the light, beautiful light,
    Come where the dew-drops of mercy are bright;
    Shine all around us by day and by night—Jesus, the Light of the world.

    Arranged further with sixteenth rests by Patricia Snyder Dustin
    Sung at Whitestone Mennonite Church by Octet
    Christmas 2009
    Contact: Martha Hershberger, Hesston, KS

Spiritual Reflection

Thank you Jesus, for
>the Bread you have given and now give us, and
>the Bread you promise to give us.

Thank you Jesus, for
>the Truth you have given and now give us, and
>the Truth that you promise to give us through your Holy Spirit.

Thank you Jesus, for
>the Life you have given and now give us, and
>the Life you promise us eternally.

Praise be to the Father, the Son, and the Holy Spirit,
>May your Triune name be magnified
>through cross, resurrection, exaltation
>lifted up so all might come and continue to believe
>>Jesus is the Christ;
>>Messiah is Jesus.

Jesus, thank you for this Gospel gift of light, life, and love!

>Yours by grace upon grace,

>Willard

John 9

Blindness and Sight: Who Is Jesus?

Nuggets

The location and Light Festival continues as context. This chapter then recounts Jesus' sixth *sign*: Jesus heals a man born blind. Sight and light are key themes, as well as their converse responses: unbelief and blindness.

The new narrative characters are the blind man and his parents. Those opposing Jesus' healing on the Sabbath (v. 16) are the accusing Pharisees and Jews.

Drama Dialogue

Consider this skit for presentation on John 9
(presented at Belmont Mennonite Church, 2011)
In the skit, note the progressive faith of the blind man.

The Man Born Blind
Based on John 9:1-41

Written by Jen Helmuth Shenk (used with permission)
Inspired by Andrew Lund and *The Message*

Cast

Narrator	Mother
Jesus	Woman
Blind man	Neighbor

■■

(Blind Man begins sitting down, as narrator reads, banging cup, begging, blind; both blind man and Jesus act out what narrator is reading)

Narrator: Jesus was walking along one day. He saw a man who was born blind. People wanted to know whose sin had caused this man's blindness - his sin, or the sin of his parents. But Jesus said God would be glorified through what was about to happen. He spat on the ground, made mud and put it on the man's eyes. Then he told him to go and wash it off in the pool of Siloam.

(*Man goes and washes his face comes back seeing. Jesus exits*)

Narrator: This caused a bit of a ruckus with the neighbors.

Neighbor: Hey (*nudges friend*)... Isn't that the same guy who used to sit around begging? It looks just like him, and as far as I know, he doesn't have a long-lost twin. Never mind, it can't be. This guy isn't blind. The other guy who begs all the time can't see a thing. (*to the man*) Hey, you! What's your name?

Blind Man: Who me?

Woman: (*does a double take*) Did you see that? He looked at us straight in the face! It can't be the same guy, but it looks like him. What do you think? Ask him!

Neighbor: (*to the man*) Look... err.... are you that blind fellow? You know, the one who used to sit around here begging?

Blind Man: That's me!

Woman: So how is it that you can see now?

Man: The man they call Jesus put some mud on my eyes, told me to go to the pool and wash. So I went and washed, and now I can see.

Woman: So where is this man they call Jesus?

Blind Man: (*shrugs, looks around*) I don't know.

Narrator:	It wasn't just the neighbors who found this all puzzling. It didn't go down well with the religious people either. You see Jesus had done this on the holy day, the Sabbath, when people weren't expected to do any work whatsoever... let alone perform miracles. So they brought the man before the Pharisees, and grilled him to pieces. Starting now! (*puts on glasses, picks up a gavel, places the Blind Man at the "witness stand" and bangs the gavel as the "court" comes to order*)
	(*to the man, rapid fire questions*) How can you see again?
Blind Man:	The man they call Jesus put mud on my eyes. He told me to wash in the Pool of Siloam, so I did. After that, I could see.
Narrator:	What kind of man is he?
Blind Man:	I'm not sure. I would guess he is a prophet.
Narrator:	You would *guess?* We're not getting anywhere with you. I would like to call my next witness, this man's mother! (*to woman*) Starting now. (*bangs the gavel*) Is that man (*pointing*) your son?
Mother:	He is.
Narrator:	Was he born blind?
Mother:	Yes, he was - I should know. I am his mother, after all.
Narrator:	Just answer the question and spare the attitude. How is it he can see now?
Mother:	I plead the fifth.
Narrator:	So how can we find out?

Mother:	Ask him. He's old enough. He can speak for himself.
Narrator:	(*sigh, exasperated*). Okay. Second round. I now call the first witness back to the stand! (*to the man*) Remember God is your witness, blah blah blah, the whole truth and nothing but the truth, etcetera, etcetera. Okay, now. We know this man they call Jesus is a sinner since he broke the law by healing on the Sabbath. Do you agree?
Blind Man:	I don't know if he's a sinner or not. All I know is I once was blind. But now I see!
Narrator:	So how exactly did he (*pantomimes air quotes*) "HEAL" you? What did he do to you? How did he open your eyes?
Blind Man:	I've told you already. Why do you want to hear it again? Do you want to become a disciple of his too?
Narrator:	Watch it. I'm the one asking the questions here. (*aside*) Strike his last comment from the record! Now. (*clenched teeth*) Please simply ANSWER the questions—with STATEMENTS. Back to this man, Jesus. Where does he come from?
Blind Man:	Now that is remarkable! You don't know where he comes from, yet he opened my eyes. You said earlier that Jesus is a sinner; but you know as well as I do that God doesn't listen to sinners. Nobody has ever heard of someone opening the eyes of a man born blind. If Jesus were not from God, he could do nothing.
Neighbor:	What does he know? He's nothing but a sinner!
Woman:	He's nothing but dirt! Do you hear how he mocks us? Throw this man out of court!

(court scene ends, Narrator back on stool)

Narrator: Jesus heard about the commotion, that they had thrown the man out, and so he went to find him. Let's see what happens next.

Jesus: Do you believe in the Son of Man?

Blind Man: Point him out to me, sir, so that I can believe in him.

Jesus: You're looking right at him. Don't you recognize my voice?

Blind Man: *(awestruck)* Master! I believe! *(falling on knees in worship)*

Jesus: I came into the world to bring everything into the clear light of day, making all the distinctions clear, so that those who have never seen will see, and those who have made a great pretense of seeing, will be exposed as blind.

Narrator: Some Pharisees who were with him heard him say this and asked if Jesus was calling *them* blind. In response, Jesus said,

Jesus: *(addressing audience)* If you are truly blind, you would be blameless. But since you claim to see everything so well, you're accountable for every fault and failure.

Blind Man: *(first addressing Jesus, then gradually turning to face front)* I used to be blind; now I can see. Now I can see. I...can *(closes eyes and bows head)*...see.

Poetry

1. The Man Born Blind

You have no notion what darkness is,
You whose eyes are closed only when you choose.
But my eyes had never seen light
until that day he touched them, and they came alive.

I remember my parents arguing long into the night—
Whose fault it was. And why?
What had they done to deserve this?
Thinking I was asleep.

    *****

It was his disciples who saw me,
Starting yet another argument,
As though blindness made me deaf and invisible.

I had heard it all a thousand times before.
The religious have always treated me as a problem
To be solved.

But he seemed uninterested in their debates.
That was when the unthinkable happened.

There was a warm stirring in my eyes
And a kind voice saying,
"Go, wash the mud from your eyes."

My first sight was the water.
The joy I experienced
Cannot be described.

Thinking my blindness a curse,
It never occurred to anyone I might be healed.

Afterwards
People asked me to explain.

It seemed strange to ask, "Why?"
When one can see.

(Kauffman 2000: 87-88; with permission)

2. *QuakerPsalm* 7, by George Fox, "Now the Lord Has Opened to Me"

Now the Lord has opened to me
by his invisible power
how everyone is enlightened
by Christ's divine light.

I see it shine through all
and they that believe in it
come out of condemnation
and into the Light of Life

And become children of God,
but they that hate it,
and do not believe in it.
are condemned by it,

though they make a profession of Christ.
I see in that Light and Spirit
which was before Scripture was given forth,
and which led the holy men of God to give them forth;

That all must come to that Spirit,
if they will know God or Christ,
or the Scriptures aright.
All must come to the Spirit
if they will know!

(George Fox, *QuakerPsalms: A Book of Devotions* 7, p. 11;
used with permission, Foundation Publications)

Song

Several songs express desire for God to open our eyes to see Jesus.

1. The one is a chorus:
   Open my eyes, Lord,
   I want to see Jesus. (*repeat several times*)

2. The second is "Open my eyes, that I may see"
   Open my eyes, that I may see
   glimpses of truth thou has for me.
   Place in my hands the wonderful key
   that shall unclasp, and set me free.
   Silently now I wait for thee,
   ready, my God, thy will to see.
   Open my eyes, illumine me, Spirit divine!

   Each of the four stanzas ends respectively with:
   "Open my: eyes/ears/heart/mind, illumine me, Spirit divine!"
   (*Hymnal: A Worship Book* 517; Clara H. Scott, 1895)

3. Another song petitions Jesus to "Come and be light for our eyes"
   (*Sing the Journey* 5).

   Refrain:
   Come and be light for our eyes
       be the air we breathe,
       be the voice we speak!
   Come be the song we sing,
       be the path we seek!

   Stanzas
           Your life was given;
               food for all people,
           body and blood,
               new life in our midst!
           Death is no longer,
               life is the future;
           Jesus, Messiah,
               name of all names.

We hold your presence,
        risen forever!
Your name now names us
        people of God!
Filled with your vision,
        people of mission,
 healing, forgiving;
        light for the world!

 Lead us to justice,
        light in the darkness;
singing, proclaiming
        Jesus is Lord!
Teach us to speak, and
        help us to listen
for when your truth and
        our dreams embrace!

Text and Music, David Haas
©1985 with GIA permission

Art

Figure 5: Jesus Heals the Blind Man.

Website: "Street Jesus" (artist source unknown)

How do the features of this image help you interact with the story in John 9? What role does light play in this story? Notice 9:5 as the context of Jesus' healing this blind man.

Story: Disability and Witness

A Laotian evangelist, Kuaying Teng, says most East Asian cultures view disability as the result of someone's sin, possibly back a few generations. Teng grew up in Laos and had a disability from birth: he couldn't walk until he was ten years old. His ten siblings, all younger than he, told him he would never be able to do anything in life and no woman would ever marry him. His culture put the same questions to him that the disciples put to Jesus: who sinned, this man or his parents?

Teng's story has similarity to that in John 9. His life was touched by Jesus, through learning to know Mennonite Central Committee workers in his country. He came to belief in Jesus as Savior and peacemaker, yielding his life to serve him. He too, like the man born blind, has stood trial numerous times for his faith, including numerous times in prison. But like the writer of Philippians he is filled with joy not only in knowing Christ but by being able to share in Jesus' sufferings (3:10). He lives in Ontario with his wife and four children, works for Mennonite Mission Network, and goes to Laos frequently to evangelize and encourage Christian believers. In autumn 2009, at the Laos' government's invitation, he went to witness on what Mennonites believe. The Laos government has made *only* the Mennonite church legal among the Christian groups. But Teng did not think the government fully understood what Mennonites believe, but thinks only of the good things done by MCC. For the sake of truth, he felt he has to tell more about belief in Jesus. Does he fear being put in prison again, we asked him in Sunday school class? He said no, because he has a Canadian passport, and in the past prison sentences arose from local opposition against him, not from the central government. Like Paul he has learned that he can witness in prison also.

Teng has a walking disability, with one leg shorter than the other. Teng tells stories of what that means for him in his culture. People watch him from behind, but he turns and begins relationships. This sometimes leads to friendships, and belief in Christ.

While Teng has not been cured of his disability, he has been healed. He radiates shalom, bearing witness to Jesus as his Savior worldwide in his travels in North America and East Asia.

See *Mennonite Weekly Review*, August 8, 2011, p. 6, reporting on Teng's ministry.

On disability, see Swartley 2012: 162-72.

John 10

Jesus: I am the Good Shepherd

Nuggets

This chapter is oriented to two Feasts: Booths/Tabernacles (September) and Dedication (December). Jesus' teachings on the Good Shepherd occur in Jerusalem.

Jesus as the Good or True Shepherd contrasts to false shepherds (see Ezekiel 34 for analogy) who are thieves and hirelings. In John they represent the deaf and blind leaders as portrayed in John (some Pharisees and other Jewish leaders).

Meditation

In his engaging book, *Images of Jesus*, Anselm Grün (79) begins his meditation on "Jesus the good shepherd" with an arresting description:

> With the image of the good shepherd Jesus expresses the deep longing of men and women in the ancient world. The Jews saw God as the true shepherd who leads his people. At God's command Moses was the shepherd and leader of his people. The Greeks knew of the shepherd who stands in a large garden and carries a sheep on his shoulder. The garden recalls paradise. The Greeks associated their longing for a whole world with the shepherd. For many cultures the shepherd is a caring father figure, an image of God's fatherly care for men and women.
>
> The early Christians took over the longings of Israel and Greece. Like God, Jesus is the shepherd who leads his people to life. The Greeks associated the figure of the good shepherd with Orpheus, the divine singer. His song tamed wild animals and restored the dead to life. He is usually depicted in an idyllic landscape surrounded by sheep and lions. Orpheus also appears again among the early Christians as Jesus. Jesus is the divine singer who with his works tames the wildness in us and restores the dead to life. When in the Gospel of John Jesus calls himself the good shepherd he addresses all the images of shepherds that slumber in the human soul as archetypical images of salvation.

Song

1. Inspiring "Shepherd" songs in the *Hymnal: A Worship Book* are: "Gentle Shepherd, come and lead us" (352); "Savior, like a shepherd lead us" (355); "The Lord's my shepherd" (578) [cf. *Sing the Story* (99)]. An appropriation of the theme to our life's journey is "My Shepherd will supply my need" (589). A favorite of mine is "In heavenly love abiding" (*Hymnal: A Worship Book* 613; text by Anna L. Waring, 1850):

> *Stanzas 2 and 3*
> Wherever he may guide me, no want shall turn me back.
> My Shepherd is beside me, and nothing can I lack.
> His wisdom ever waketh, his sight is never dim,
> He knows the way he taketh,
> and I will walk with him (2x).
>
> Green pastures are before me, which yet I have not seen.
> Bright skies will soon be o'er me, where darkest clouds have been.
> My hope I cannot measure, my path to life is free,
> My Savior has my treasure,
> and he will walk with me (2x).

Art
Figure 6a. Jesus the Good Shepherd

(Website image, artist source unknown)

Figure 6b. Jesus the Good Shepherd

The Good Shepherd, Icon design by Rev. Pachomius Meade, O.S.B
© The Printery House, Conception Abbey, Conception, MO. USA.
Used with permission.

What do you see in this icon of the good shepherd? The IC in upper right is the contraction for *Jesus* and the XC on left is the contraction for *Christ*, with first and last letters of each word in uncial-cap print.

John 11:1–12:11

Jesus' Climactic Sign:

Lazarus' Death, Resurrection, and Aftermath

Nuggets

The setting for the events of this Scriptural unit is Bethany, two miles from Jerusalem, and in the home of Martha, Mary, and Lazarus, and its environs, for a graveyard. The key event is Lazarus's illness and death. Jesus responds in two stages: a four-day delay and then coming to their home to magnify God's glory: *so that the Son of God may be glorified through it* (v. 4).

Jesus' *I AM...* claim and Martha's confession are memorable: *Jesus said to her, "I am the resurrection and the life. Those who believe in me, even though they die, will live, and everyone who lives and believes in me will never die. Do you believe this?" She said to him, "Yes, Lord, I believe that you are the Messiah, the Son of God, the one coming into the world." (vv. 25-27).*

Other memorable events are:

- Empathizing with Mary's weeping, *Jesus wept.*
- Jesus raises Lazarus, a foreshadowing of Jesus' resurrection.
- Because of Jesus' miracles and popularity, the Jews fear the Romans will come and destroy *our holy place and our nation* (v. 48), followed by Caiaphas's proposal, which as unbeknown prophecy ironically forecasts Jesus' death.
- Authorities are on the watch for Jesus.
- Mary anoints the feet of Jesus and Judas protests (12:1-8).
- The chief priests seek to kill Lazarus, a life-size witness to Jesus.

Context: One puzzle of John's Gospel is authorship. As noted in the "Introduction," Lazarus may have contributed to the Gospel's authorship. Here are the salient points of evidence, in addition to John 11:3 and 5.

P. Much of John's Gospel is based in Jerusalem. The Bethany home of Mary, Martha, and Lazarus appears to have been Jesus' Jerusalem home.

Q. The Synoptic Gospels record that Jesus' disciples deserted him before the crucifixion. But John says the Beloved Disciple and Jesus' mother are standing beneath the cross. This implies Lazarus was not one of the Twelve. Jesus' command that the Beloved Disciple receive Jesus' mother into his home makes sense if the home is only two miles away (the distance between Bethany and Jerusalem).

R. The owner of the house customarily reclined with the chief guest, in this case Jesus. The Beloved Disciple sits next to Jesus at the Supper. Thus, Lazarus fulfills his host role.

S. Because Lazarus lived near Jerusalem it was likely he (not a Galilean disciple, John) who would have been familiar enough to enter into the chief priest's house (18:15). Also an important second century source ascribes to the author of the Gospel priestly identity!

T. Peter's question regarding the Beloved Disciple's death in 21:21-23 makes sense if Lazarus was the Beloved Disciple.

Meditation on Lazarus #1

The Resurrection of Lazarus
The door rolled back,
and forth he came
called by the one
whose voice he knew.

"Unbind!" he heard,
and then could feel
hands tearing away
what held him fast.

How strange again
to feel the sun
and breathe the air,
fresh from the field.

He didn't want
to come, but knew
he must. For death
would take his Lord.

Then how'd they know
that life was more,
extending from both
sides the door,
    called death;
that on both sides
embraced and lived,
both life and death
belong to God?
    And so,
forever, still,
we hear the call
to be unbound
from fear of death -
    and life.

Arthur Freeman, 1992 (with permission).

75

Meditation on Lazarus #2

From the mystery of the womb
To the silence of the tomb
    Life moves through its stages;
What was gained
    Slips through our grasp
Thrust upon the mercies of
    existence beyond our control
We are amazed to find life
    sustained by God.

Then we realize that
    living is not only birth and growth
dying is not only life's
    final stillness.

Dying is that which
    weighs life down,
keeps life from unfolding,
    binds it,
drains its possibilities.

Dying is
    fearing to live,
    staring upon life with empty eyes,
    seeing nothing.

Living is finding
    the Source of life
    Who gifts our existence
    and sustains us.

Arthur Freeman, 1983 (with permission).

Song

1. **When Jesus learned his friend had died**:
   Adam Tice composed lyrics, "When Jesus learned his friend had died," and selected a tune for them. The hymn focuses on Jesus' raising of Lazarus, giving him life, echoing 1:4 in the Prologue ("in him was life") and prefiguring Jesus' own death and resurrection,

   Stanza 4:
   When loved ones fall to death's dread sleep,
       like Jesus, we can freely weep
       and give our anguished breath.
   With Christ, we turn to face the cross
   where he confronted pain and loss
       and rose, defeating death.

   886.886 Suggested tune: CHAPEL (repeat the last line of each verse) ©2003 AML Tice; with GIA permission; see also the full text in *Vision: A Journal for Church and Theology*, Fall 2007, p. 87).

2. **Mary of Bethany's anointing the feet of Jesus**

   A woman poured her jar of rich perfume

   A woman poured her jar of rich perfume
   All over Jesus' feet with loving care
   She knelt as fragrance quickly filled the room
   She touched his feet, and washed them with her hair.

   She washed his feet, not thinking of the cost—
   The best she had, the woman freely gave
   His love was more to her than money lost;
   Her gift anointed Jesus for his grave.

   10.10.10.10 Suggested tunes: PENETENTIA, FIELD
   ©June 4, 2004, AML Tice
   Adam M. L. Tice, with GIA permission.

Art: Figure 7

Martha: "I believe you are the Messiah, the Son of God" (John 11:27).

Jesus responds to Martha's confession with the words of this art image. Contemplate this art portrayal. Notice how light-waves merge toward and into the cross-resurrection. Jesus raising Lazarus prefigures his own resurrection (John 20). How great was Martha's role in John's Gospel! Identify with her emotions in her encounter with Jesus.

Christianity 201website; artist source unknown

It is striking that women make major confessions of Jesus' identity toward the end of the Gospel's three major units: the Samaritan woman in chapter 4; Martha in chapter 11; Mary Magdalene in chapter 20! What might this say about John's Gospel?!

John 12:12-50

The Final Scene in Jesus' Public Ministry

Nuggets

Jesus' triumphal entry into Jerusalem climaxes his public ministry. It occurs five days before the final Passover. This is followed by another extraordinary event: Greeks come and ask to see Jesus (12:20-22).

This prompts Jesus' response, *"The hour has come...,"* for Jesus' glorification. Jesus unveils the meaning of this *hour*, using the image of a grain of wheat falling into the ground, dying, and bearing fruit. Here we see Jesus' Gethsemane-type struggle and hear Jesus' call to walk in the light.

Responses of belief and unbelief dot the narrative landscape of John's Gospel. Jesus now explains the Jews' unbelief (12:36b-43), quoting from Isaiah. Then we are also told that *many of the authorities believed in him* (v. 42).

The curtain closes on Jesus' public ministry with his final summative appeal (44-50), beckoning his hearers to flee the darkness and follow the light.

Thus Jesus fulfills his Father's commandment, to give eternal life!

Meditation

1. Some aspects of Jesus' entry into Jerusalem are reenacted in many churches each Palm Sunday. What is your response? The dissonance between this apparent triumph, with crowds welcoming Jesus as King, and the crucifixion of Jesus as "King of the Jews" just five days later shocks. Picture in your mind and heart these two scenes. Imagine the trauma Jesus' disciples experienced (see Chapter 20 for reflection on trauma).

2. The coming of the Gentiles to see Jesus marks the turning point from *"my hour has not yet come"* to *"my hour has come!"* See the entry in *John*, "The Text in Biblical Context:" "The Greeks Come to See Jesus." Note the similar shift that occurs in Mark, Matthew, and Luke when Gentiles are included into Jesus' ministry. Mission is

thus the heart of the gospel story. Mission embodies peacemaking, since Gentiles were enemies of the Jews. Gary M. Burge writes,

It has become commonplace to say that in America, 11:00 A.M. on Sunday is the most segregated hour of the week. If we do not understand the radical mandate of Jesus or his willingness to take the social risk of being with Greeks *in the Jerusalem temple,* we do not comprehend Jesus' extreme love for the world. At the same time, we have to understand the risk. After hearing about the Greeks, Jesus immediately speaks of sacrifice and the cross. The same risks pertain to us who likewise see Jesus' vision and take a parallel social risk of being with "Greeks" *in the local evangelical church* (359).

Rachel Epp Miller (2004 AMBS student) applies the Greek's inquiry to churches today:

The widening ministry of Jesus inspires us to be a global community of believers. It also inspires us to open our doors in our neighborhoods to welcome the diversity of God's family into our fellowship.

This is not without risk… While this task is not without risk, it is also not without hope. Jesus risked everything, but did so knowing that God's purpose was bigger than what was seen in the struggle, that God's promise was life through the glorification of God's Son. This is the hope and promise that we continue to carry today. We can risk to enter into the challenges and blessings of a diverse church, knowing that Jesus has torn down the dividing walls between us (Eph 2:14) and that Jesus will draw all of us and all creation to himself (12:32; cf. Eph 1:10). This is our hope and challenge as Christ's church today. (used with permission)

3. As we come to this pivotal turn in John's Gospel we are faced with varying responses to Jesus. As Gospel readers we are challenged to choose our own response to Jesus:
    - Chief priests: get rid of Jesus
    - Pharisees: fear Jesus' popularity
    - Crowd: enthusiastic, but later cry, "crucify"
    - Disciples: understand later
    - Greeks (Gentiles): want to see Jesus

Or, perhaps, we identify with the Bethany family, Martha, Mary, and Lazarus, Jesus' friends who cared for him and received his love. When we say *yes* to follow Jesus (12:26) we receive Jesus' commandment from the Father: *eternal life* (12:50). For extensive discussion of eternal life in John's Gospel, see the Essay in *John* on Eternal Life.

Song

1. Three hymns in the *Hymnal: A Worship Book* (237, 238, and 239) stress different aspects of Jesus' triumphal entry. The first fits best with Matthew (the only Gospel to record the praise of the children); the second, with Mark; and the third, with John. Reflect upon these lines of stanza 1, 2, and 4 from #239:

    > Ride on, ride on in majesty,
    > as all the crowds "Hosanna!" cry,
    > through waving branches slowly ride,
    > O Savior, to be crucified.

    > Ride on, ride on in majesty,
    > in lowly pomp ride on to die.
    > O Christ, your triumph now begin
    > with captured death and conquered sin!

    > Ride on, ride on in majesty,
    > in lowly pomp ride on to die.
    > Bow your meek head to mortal pain,
    > then take, O God, your pow'r and reign.
    > (used with permission, ©Hope Publishing Company)

2. Another song that fits John's emphases of Jesus' entry into Jerusalem is "The King of Glory," *Sing and Rejoice* 122, notably stanzas 1 and 4:
    > *Refrain*
    > The King of glory comes,
    > the nation rejoices.
    > Open the gates before Him,
    > lift up your voices.

Stanzas 1 and 4
Who is the King of glory;
how shall we call Him?
He is Emmanuel,
the promised of ages.

He gave His life for us,
the pledge of salvation,
He took upon Himself
the sins of the nation.
(©Willard F. Jabusch; inaccessible)

Overview and Meditation
Life and Truth, Glory and Love

Many commentators structure John as follows:

John 1:1-18	Prologue
John 1–12	The Book of Signs
John 13–20	The Book of Glory
John 21	Epilogue

This is helpful to comprehend the whole. In the first half of John (*eternal*) *life/living* occurs many times (54), with most in John 1–12. both *truth* and *truly* also occur often in this part, with key verses 1:17 and 8:32; Jesus often begins speaking with *very truly. Glory* and *love* permeate John 13–20 (36 times in 13–21, but only 8 times in 1–12).

However, the theme of glory permeates the entire book, beginning in the Prologue (1:14) and at the end of Jesus' first week of ministry (2:11). See *John* (the Believers Church Bible Commentary) for extended discussion of "Glory" at several places:

1. "The Glory Drama of Scripture" in the Prologue
2. "Cross and Glorification" in John 12; John correlates cross with glory
3. "Glorification" in "The Text in Biblical Context," John 19.

   John 13 and 17 intensify the theme of glory, as this depiction of the main themes of John 13–17 shows (the overlap of themes progresses, as this diagram illustrates):

	13:31-35 (36-38)	14:1–15:17	15:18–17:26
(1)	Glorification	World	Conflict Tribulation
(2)	Departure (absence)	Paraclete (presence)	Unity & Mutual Indwelling
(3)	Love commandment	"Obey my word" and "abide in my love"	Love, unity, *glory*, that the world may believe

The movement is down for column 1, up for column 2, and down for column 3. Hence the theme in the third position (3) comes first in 14:1–15:17. New dimensions of exhortation appear as the narrative progresses. *Glory* and love bookend this section.

To God be the glory!
We thank you, Jesus Christ, for manifesting God's glory.
Come Paraclete (Holy Spirit),
to empower us to glorify the Father and the Son.

John 13:1-38

Jesus Begins "Farewell"

Nuggets

Jesus' "Farewell Speech" is on the evening *before* the Passover meal (this differs from the Synoptic Gospels, which view the Thursday evening meal as the Passover). In John, Jesus dies on Friday as the *Lamb* to be sacrificed and eaten, presumably at the Passover meal (cf. 6:53-58).

The five-chapter Farewell (chs. 13-17) begins with Jesus washing his disciples' feet at his last supper with them. Footwashing forgives sin and renews baptism (see Commentary) and calls to humble service.

A new (?) character: the beloved disciple, leaning on Jesus' breast, emerges in a significant role in the narrative. Judas is identified as the one who will "hand Jesus over" to the authorities seeking to kill him.

Jesus gives a new commandment, *love one another*, central to discipleship in John's Gospel and 1 John. Peter pledges loyalty at all costs, but Jesus says, "you can't do it yet; you will deny me three times."

Meditation

1. Jesus' self-giving and glory at the Last Supper prefigures Jesus' death:

   Your glory was hidden from human eyes for most of your life. But now, at this last supper, the moment is near when the veil of time will be lifted. Then will the glory of eternity explode in the battered frame of your bruised face and broken body. For our sake you hide your might and majesty. You relinquish freely and joyfully the glory that was yours before the world began. (van Kaam: 71)

2. At the Lausanne Forum on World Evangelization in Pattaya, Thailand, in 2004, thirty "issue groups" were formed for discussion, with reporting back at the end. Group 22, focusing on reconciliation

85

across societal barriers and polarization, washed feet to demonstrate:

> ...when the time for our report came, we set up on the convention floor twelve people with basins and towels. Then as two people narrated what happened in our group during the week, the twelve people washed each other's feet: a Catholic priest, an Orthodox priest, and an evangelical pastor; an Israeli and a Palestinian; a black, a white and an Asian American; Hutu and Tutsi; male and female.
>
> At the end of the presentation, the polite silence was interrupted by a standing ovation...
>
> We did not meet to fix the many divisions and conflicts represented by the members of our group...(but) what was poignantly revealed and confirmed to us in the gesture of footwashing was the nature and mission of the church in reconciliation (Katongole and Rice, 110-12).

Song

1. Jesus loves *his own* to the end (v. 1). Meditate on the words and be inspired by the tune and harmony of two great hymns in *Hymnal: A Worship Book*: "O Love of God" (326), especially stanzas 4, 5, and 6; and "O Power of love" (593), especially stanza 3:

    To thee my heart and life be given;
    thou art in truth my highest good.
    For me thy sacred side was riven,
    for me was shed thy precious blood.
    O thou who art the world's salvation,
    be thine my love and adoration.

2. The song, "He came down" (*Sing the Journey* 31) strongly affirms Jesus' gift in this chapter, in the stanza with "love:" "He came down, that we may have love" (sung 3 times). To accentuate footwashing, sing "He knelt down, that we may have love." This links the first and last parts of John 10: footwashing and Jesus' command to love one another.

3. Look through the hymn book of your choice to find hymns on footwashing (see *Hymnal: A Worship Book* 449-452, as well as 305, 307, 310). How do these hymns connect with your sense of the

significance of footwashing? Footwashing has had different meanings for me in different settings and circumstances of my life or the life of the one with whom I washed feet. It has been most meaningful to me when it connects to my human experience, or that of my partner(s). In one such case it enacted forgiveness in response to confession of sin.

4. A meaningful hymn to me is "Jesus took a towel" and washed my feet. Meditate on the lyrics of this hymn in the *Hymnal: A Worship Book* 449.

5. Climaxing the themes of cleansing and lowly service in the footwashing is Jesus' command to his disciples to *love one another*, the mark of their discipleship and belonging to Jesus. Meditate on the words of this hymn:

> God of love,
> light a flame of love in our hearts to you,
> a flame of love to our families and friends,
> a flame of love to our neighbors,
> a flame of love to our enemies.
>
> Light a flame of love in our hearts to all,
> from the lowliest thing that lives,
> to the Name that is highest of all. AMEN
>
> *Sing the Journey* 121

Art

Figure 8a: Jesus and his disciples at the Last Supper

As you meditate on these photos of the Last Supper and Jesus washing his disciples' feet, let your eyes see and mind perceive the holiness and sacredness of this *hour* in John. What a joy to see this reenactment, often with tears of deep emotion.

See Figure 8b for photo source and church of enactment by Kirk and Patti Lytle

Figure 8b: Jesus Washes the Disciples' Feet

In the DVD I recommended in the "Introduction" a woman, likely Mary Magdalene, is portrayed in this group as well. This matches our footwashing experiences today. Try journaling on one footwashing experience that was especially meaningful to you.

Photographs by Bruce Lehman (with permission); courtesy also of Bahia Vista Mennonite Church and Kirk and Patti Ministries. Patti, with Kirk as narrator Caleb ("Shrimp"), directed on a Sunday morning (February 2009) this powerful drama, "A Night to Remember," a "recreation" of the Last Supper and Jesus washing his disciples' feet. As the apostles take their seat (one by one) at the table, narrator Caleb tells the story of the apostle's call and his later apostolic work and martyrdom. Church members were trained by Patti and Kirk on Saturday to play their respective apostolic roles. The disciples came one by one to the foot-washing, sometimes with Jesus speaking and sometimes in silence. Powerful and unforgettable—what a worship service!

A Responsive Reading for Footwashing

L: The love of Christ has gathered us as one,
   to remember Jesus Christ, the Son of God,
   who loved his own until the end.
P: **In his great, unselfish love,**
   the Master who calmed the storms
   and turned water into wine,
   stooped to do a servant's duty
   and washed his disciples' feet.
L: When we are gathered here,
   let us be drawn together by his passion.
   Let no pride dismiss his model,
   let no love be less than his.
P: **Let us follow Christ's example**
   and demonstrate the service
   by which we show love for one another.
   For by this, the world will know
   that we are Christ's disciples,
   if we love one another.

Arlene M. Mark, in *Words for Worship*, #254.
Based on John 13:34-35.

Story

In Franconia Mennonite Conference where I grew up, we practiced footwashing twice annually in a three-event process. On a scheduled Sunday in spring (close to Good Friday) and fall, we had "counsel" meeting after the service, at which time all members were to greet and be greeted by the minister or bishop. If anything needed "cleansing" that was the time to "confess sin" and make it right. Then the following Saturday afternoon was the Footwashing Service, which enacted the cleansed life and symbolized servant-life to Christ and to one another. The next day was Communion, celebrating cleansing and humble service.

In contrast, the Brethren in Christ combine Love Feast, Footwashing, and Communion in one most meaningful service.

The rent we pay for living

When he had finished washing their feet, he put on his clothes
and returned to his place. "Do you understand
what I have done for you?" he asked them.
"You call me 'Teacher' and 'Lord,' and rightly so, for that is what I am.
Now that I, your Lord and Teacher, have washed your feet,
you also should wash one another's feet.
I have set you an example that you should do as I have done for you.
I tell you the truth, no servant is greater than his master,
nor is a messenger greater than the one who sent him.
Now that you know these things, you will be blessed if you do them.
—John 13:12-17

I came back from a trip to do hurricane cleanup and reconstruction in Mobile, Ala., and I couldn't stop talking about it.

****

...service takes me away from my everyday world and gives me a new perspective on life. I heard stories from people who lived through the hurricane but hadn't been featured on national news, even though spending six hours on a floating dining room table with two mammoth Great Danes would have been well worth the listen. The Way of Life congregation in Mobile bestowed extraordinary Southern hospitality on us, not only preparing our food, but also washing our evening dishes.

The house was dedicated on January 16 because that was the 20th anniversary of the establishment of the Martin Luther King Jr. federal holiday. The original vision for a day honoring Dr. King was for it to be a day of service a time when people from all walks of life could join together to address important community issues. Working alongside individuals of all ages, races, and backgrounds, Dr. King encouraged Americans to come together to strengthen communities, alleviate poverty, and acknowledge dignity and respect for all human beings. Service, he realized, was the great equalizer. "Everybody can be great, because everybody can serve," he reminded us.

Why does service matter? My young niece said, "You should say doing service is important because it gives you a warm and fuzzy feeling." Feeling content in oneself is no small thing, but doing service gets me beyond saying I believe in Jesus to acting on that belief by doing as Jesus taught us to do. When Jesus washed the feet of his disciples he not only showed us the importance of service, but he put it into words: "You also should wash one another's feet. . . . Now that you know these things, you will be blessed if you do them" (John 13:1-17).

I washed windows rather than feet, but I did that as my way of acting on Jesus words. Mostly, of course, it is we who serve who are changed. I'd guess Jesus, master changer of hearts, knows that.

Serve well!

Susan Mark Landis (2010: 33-34)
Seasoned with Peace, Winter
(used with permission)

John 13:35–16:33

Overview of Jesus' Farewell Discourse

Nuggets

Numerous themes recur, and tumble over one another in Jesus' farewell discourse. I arrange them in a chiastic pattern, with the promised *Paraclete* at the center and assurances and peace as the bookends:

a Assurances for the future
  b Departure (I am going away) and
        Consolation (I will not leave you alone)
    c Injunctions to love
      d Keep my commandment(s)
        e "Abide in me" ("in my love") as branches in the vine
          f Fivefold promise of the *Paraclete*/Holy Spirit to come
        e' Jesus, the way to (know) the Father: mutual glorification
      d' Ask, and it will be done (14:13-14; 15:7, 16; 16:23-24)
    c' Warnings of the world's hatred (persecution)
  b' Promise of Jesus' return
a' Gift of peace

In this portion of Scripture Jesus promises the coming of the *Paraclete* (Spirit of Truth and Holy Spirit) five times. Each time some aspect of the *Paraclete's* work is described.

Meditation on Spiritual Formation

1. Thomas Brodie (429-33) see here three stages of spiritual formation:

   Stage 1, chs. 13-14: *cleansing*—"the believer and the world's evil are intermingled, and the task is to drive out the root of the evil." Here the footwashing is interpreted as cleansing from sin. Judas's exit is also symbolic of this separation of evil from the disciple band. John emphasizes Satan's role in Judas's action.

   Stage 2, chs. 15-16: *purification*—"when the root of evil has been driven out and God is purifying the believer, there is a certain withdrawal from the world, a painful struggle to be free from all that chains the heart." This is accompanied by dual literary emphases: God's purifying and the hating action of the world: "a key function of the picture of the world's hatred is to highlight the idea that in following Christ, in drawing close to God, one must go through a stage of letting go of the world, a stage of separation, and one must place one's roots where they truly belong—in God. The world, ...challenged or spurned, tends to feel resentment, and from this comes an antipathy, a hatred."

Stage 3, ch. 17: *sanctification*—"when one's identity in God has been firmly established, there is a return to the world—not as something to be either exploited or idolized, but as something in which, despite its evil, one works for faith and understanding (...esp. 17:11, 15, 21, 23)."

Brodie perceives a similar progression in the "Peace" texts in 14:27 and 16:33.

> John 14:27: "*Peace I leave with you; my peace I give to you. I do not give to you as the world gives. Do not let your hearts be troubled, and do not let them be afraid.*"John 16:33: "*I have said this to you, so that in me you may have peace. In the world you face persecution. But take courage; I have conquered the world!*"

These texts respond to two complementary scenes: the beloved disciple's entry into the narrative and Jesus' giving the new commandment: love one another. In the first stage (ch. 14), the disciples are trying to see and admit the divine presence, there is a related twofold conclusion: "first, there is a picture of spirit-based peace (14:25-27b), and then there is a picture of all that threatens that peace (14:27c-31)...The overall picture of chaps. 14–15 ....is of the development of a love, or of a love-related peace, which is present but threatened" (434).

In the second stage (16:4b-33) there is both a deepening of the "Spirit-led discernment of truth" and a change in the image of peace:

> ...the believer now understands the Father's love directly (16:26-27)...the negative does not win; one is not alone and beaten. On the contrary,... the distress of the world, though very real, has been overcome, and in the presence of the Father there is a deep peace. Hence the final phrase: 'I have defeated the world' (Brodie: 435).

In John 13-17 there "is a gradual disentangling of the forces of good and evil": first, interwoven (betrayer in the midst); second, a clear division

(Judas gone and Peter's denial foretold); third, clearly separated (chs. 14-16); and finally, "evil has been left aside" (ch. 17). The whole discourse is about "Jesus' God-oriented battle against evil and the believer's consequent journey to God" (Brodie: 435).

Strikingly, these two interpretations, political (see "Political Perspective" in the "Introduction" to the Commentary) and spiritual, do not compete with each other, but reinforce each other, as is apparent in Brodie's final "stage"! The two blend, evoking the Qumran use of *Paraclete* as one who leads the battle (see Commentary on ch. 14). This combination of the spiritual/mystical and political is vintage John.

2. A significant resource for these chapters is Marlene Kropf & Eddy Hall's book *Praying with the Anabaptists: The Secret of Bearing Fruit,* designed to foster meditation for spiritual formation. It consists of three sections:
    Part 1:   Abiding in the Vine
    Part 2:   Joined in Love
    Part 3:   Bearing Fruit
    While the meditations are mainly on John 15, some chapters focus on other parts of the Farewell Discourse. Each chapter ends pointing to some practice or prayer-testimony of a martyr, followed by a guided spiritual reflection. The meditations are enhanced by a companion cassette, "Praying with the Anabaptists," with hymns by the Chamber Singers of Eastern Mennonite University, directed by Kenneth Nafziger. Since Anabaptists often sang hymns of praise to God while in prison, awaiting their martyr-death, this musical companion is most appropriate.

3. The hymn-prayer, "Spirit of God! descend," devotes three stanzas (1, 3, and 5) to love between us and God. One of my morning meditations in July 2012 focused on Luke 10:27-30 where the young lawyer states the second commandment as the second part of what God requires to gain eternal life. This hymn seared into my heart for some reason, though my meditation included nothing about the Spirit. When I found it (*Hymnal: A Worship Book* 502), stanza 3, line 2 speaks the connection: "All, all thine own, soul, heart, and strength, and mind." The last stanza begins with "Teach me to love thee as thine angels love" and ends with "my heart an altar, and thy love the flame." Each of these stanzas nourishes a love-spirituality.

John 14:1-31

Jesus' Love;

The Way, The Truth, and The Life

Nugget

Jesus gives this speech immediately after Jesus' last supper with his disciples. Many of the themes in my chiasm in the above "Overview" of chapters 13-17 occur in this chapter.

Meditation

1. "My Father's house" in 2:16 and here again in 14:2 is an important and precious image in John. While Jesus as Son often speaks of "the Father" and sometimes "my Father," he also in this image, derived from "temple" theology in the Old Testament, speaks of *place* and *space*. Some commentators, especially Mary Coloe (see her book titles in the Bibliography) regard God's dwelling a dominant image in John. Psalm 84 is a wonderful hymn of praise for God's presence in the temple, which fulfills God's promise to David and his descendants: "I will build a house for you" (2 Sam 7). This means *God's house* will not be confined to the temple. The second Jewish temple was destroyed before John writes his Gospel. But the Gospel transforms that image into God's promise of eternally abiding in *my Father's house*, which Jesus goes to prepare for us. Praise and thanks be to God for this promise and hope! What does worship *place* and *space* mean to you?

2. The Christmas hymn, "O Holy Night," stanza 3: "His law is love, and His gospel is peace." These two declarations unite chapters 13 and 14 (see John 13:34-35 and 14:27). To what extent do you regard love and peace as flowing from the incarnate Christ?

Song

1. Rich Mullins (deceased, 1997, from an automobile accident driving to Tabor College Hillsboro, KS for a benefit concert—see http://en.wikipedia.org/wiki/Rich_Mullins), has rich song-lyrics for this Scripture:

> In my Father's house, there are many rooms. (2 times)
> And I'm going there now to prepare a place for you
> That where I am, there you may also be.
>
> If I go prepare a place for you, I will come back again. (2 times)
> You know I am the way, the truth, the life, keep my commands,
> That where I am, there you may also be.
>
> *Chorus*
> That where I am, there you may also be,
> Up where the truth, the truth will set you free.
> In the world you will have trouble, but I leave you my peace,
> That where I am, there you may also be.
>
> Remember you did not choose me, no, I have chosen you. (2x)
> The world will show you hatred; the Spirit will show you truth,
> That where I am, there you may also be.
>
> I've come down from the Father, time for me to go back up. (2x)
> One command I leave with you, love as I have loved,
> That where I am, there you may also be. *Chorus*

2. Jesus says he is the Way, the Truth, and the Life. This declaration is used appropriately in the hymn text of George Herbert. Inspired by John 14:6, George Herbert (1633), wrote these wondrous lines, set to music by Ralph Vaughan Williams (1911):

> Come, my Way, my Truth, my Life:
> such a way as gives us breath;
> such a truth as ends all strife;
> such a life as killeth death.

The third stanza fits well with John 15. It speaks of joy and love:
　　Come my Joy, my Love, my Heart:
　　such a joy as none can move;
　　such a love as none can part;
　　such a heart as joys in love.
　　(*Hymnal: A Worship Book* 587)

3. Paul Dueck's rendition of Psalm 84 and other Psalms on his Celtic and Paraguayan harps lifts the soul to enter God's presence, and assures us of God's presence with us, corporately and personally. Listen to his CDs, especially "The Lord Is My Shepherd: The Psalms." Another excellent hymn is *One Thing I Ask* (based on Psalm 27:4) by Andy Park, arranged by Jim Teel, sung by the Sarasota Mennonite Male choir at its 2011 Festival, under the direction of Lloyd Kauffman. What hymns or cantatas come to your mind as you think of dwelling with God in the place and space Jesus prepares for us, now and eternally?

Prayer

Pentecost: Receive the Spirit

Leader:	Come, Holy Spirit,
	lamplighter, midwife of change,
	comforter, disturber, inspirer, and advocate.
People:	**Come, fill the church**
	with the gifts earth
	can neither produce nor afford.
Leader:	Come, fill our lives
	with that rich mixture of peace and restlessness,
	calm and enthusiasm,
	which are hallmarks of holiness.
ALL:	*Come, promised Spirit of God,*
	find your way and make your home among us. AMEN

Sing the Story 189

John 15:1–16:4

Mutual Indwelling of Jesus and Disciples:

Abiding and Loving, Facing Hatred

Nuggets

This part of Jesus' "Farewell" is a rich resource for spiritual reflection. Every sentence counts. The key imagery is: Jesus is the true vine and the disciples are the branches; the Father is the Vine-grower. The same Greek root refers to *prune* in v.2 and *cleanse* in v. 3, which is also used for *clean* in John 13:10. This connects the cleansing of foot-washing with pruning in order to bear fruit.

The main emphases are:

- Jesus invites his disciples to *abide* (*menō*) in him as he abides in them.
- Pruning is necessary to bear fruit.
- *As the Father has loved me, so I have loved you; abide in my love* (v. 9)
- This enables Jesus' *joy* to be in us, and our *joy* to be complete.
- *Agapē* love gives one's own life for the other.
- I call you no longer servants, but *friends.*
- As the world hated Jesus, so it will hate you.
- Jesus promises to send the *Paraclete*, an Advocate from the Father,
     who will testify to Jesus.
- You will be put out of synagogues.

This chiastic arrangement ("Essay," "Chiasm" in *John*) aids meditation:

a Abide in Jesus, the true vine; disciples, the branches (1-6)
     b keep my commandments: love and bear fruit (7-10)
          c so that your joy may be full (11)
     b' keep my commandment: love, friends, fruit (12-17)
a' and a'' below contrast to a above.

a' World's hatred (18-25)
     b' promise of the Advocate (26-27)
a'' Will be put out of synagogues (16:1-4)

Call to Worship or Confession

Power of love

My command is this:
Love each other as I have loved you.
--John 15:12 (NIV 1984)

God, we confess that we fear the power of your love.
To love others as you love is to abandon our need to be first,
our quest to be the strongest,
our compulsion to stay free of danger.

Compassion means risks and change.
It opens new geographies of the spirit—and these terrify us.

We cling to what we know:
opponents to defeat,
weak people to patronize,
earth to exploit, and
interests to protect.

Unmask our illusions of safety and strength.

Draw us to the child of Bethlehem,
the suffering servant of Calvary,
the risen One whose love casts out all fear.

Breathe your wild and gentle Spirit upon us
and send us into the world with the courage to love as you Love.

Byron Rempel-Burkholder, *Seasoned with Peace* (Fall 2011: 260)
Compiled by Susan Mark Landis (used with permission)

Meditation

1. Write a personalized version of John 15:1-9. See Song texts at end of this chapter for inspiration. How are you related to the Vine, Jesus? Commune with your Redeemer-Friend, Jesus. Your reflection might begin like this: *I draw life from You, the Vine. I abide in You, Jesus, and You abide in me...* This meditation nourished me during a week of trying to resolve three distressing problems.

2. Marlene Kropf and Eddy Hall in their book *Praying with the Anabaptists: The Secret of Bearing Fruit*, is on Jesus' Farewell section in John, with extensive focus on John 15 (pp. 32-39). This prompts spiritual reflection on *abiding* in Jesus. In one meditation, they guide us in how we might think of *pruning* in order to *bear fruit*:

> With this image of pruning, Jesus gives us the secret of navigating smoothly the difficult transition between seasons of ministry [and Christian living]. If we appreciate the purpose of the pruning—greater faithfulness—we can choose not to focus on our loss. We can instead give thanks for the privilege we've enjoyed of bearing fruit for the vine in the past season and eagerly anticipate the greater fruitfulness God is preparing us for in the season to come. (61).

Since *cleanse* and *prune* derive from the same Greek root, have you ever experienced foot-washing as both cleansing and pruning? I have on several occasions. On two work days before writing this, my son and I, separated by miles, were engaged in similar tasks, picking fruit. He and his daughters picked apples from one tree rich in fruit, generating 140 quarts of applesauce. I picked blackberries from a wildly grown expansive patch, and found few berries. My son pruned his Iowan apple tree; the old dying canes in the Michigan berry patch had not been cut off, and hence the berry crop was meager. The fruit outcome: ca. 140 quarts of applesauce (more yet to be made) from one tree and 14 cups of blackberry jam from one huge patch!! Our stories connected by email over the intervening weekend.

3. "As we unite with God, we are invited into bonding rather than bondage."
   Flora Slosson Wuellner, in *Weavings*. Richard A. Kauffman Quotations, *ChrToday*, Aug. 2008: 51.

4. Jesus now addresses his disciples as friends. He names them friends because of his intimate relationship with them.

   Jesus began calling His disciples friends rather than servants because He had entrusted them with everything He had heard from His Father (John 15:15). He trusted the disciples to use the information for the good of His Father's kingdom. Although we know Jesus is our friend, can we say that we are His friends? Do we listen to Him? Or do we only want Him to listen to us? Do we want to know what's on His heart? Or do we want to tell Him what's on ours? To be a friend of Jesus, we need to listen to what He wants us to know and then use the information to bring others into friendship with him. –Julie Ackerman Link, *Our Daily Bread* (July 5, 2011).

5. Praying this text: Jesus asks us to abide in him. Jesus then also abides in us (v. 5).

   Abide in our intellect, that we may think of you.
   Abide in our intuition, that we may delight in your glory.
   Abide in our speech, that we may honor you.
   Abide in our decisions, that we may be just and merciful.
   Abide in our actions, that we may participate in the mission among and beyond us.
   Diane Zaerr Brenneman, *Words for Worship* 2, #84.

6. This is the last *I AM* with a predicate nominative in John. These metaphors connect to our human experience and yearnings. Consider your deepest felt-need among those below for further reflection and writing, extending what you began in 1 above.

Jesus comes to us in our need and says, *I AM*

Our Need	Jesus' Promise
Thirst	*I AM* Living Water for your thirsty soul.
Hunger	*I AM* the Bread of Life for your hungering spirit.
Darkness	*I AM* the Light driving out the darkness.
Caring love	*I AM* the Good Shepherd; I care for my own I will protect you and love you.
Forsaken, Dying	*I AM* the Resurrection and the Life, and I will raise you up to life on the last day.
Lost life-direction	*I AM* the Way, the Truth, and the Life.
Disconnected Fruitless	*I AM* the true Vine; you are my branches. Connected to *Me*, you will bear fruit.

What role does your community of faith play in helping you link your needs to Jesus' promises? Try this exercise with your small group.

Song

1. **Jesus is the True Vine**

    Jesus is the True Vine, all we are his branches,
    much fruit will we bear if in him we abide.
    The Father of Jesus, he is the vinedresser,
    the fruit-bearing branches with care he does prune.
    In love did he choose us, his friends has he called us,
    appointing us all to go forth and bear fruit.
    If you abide in me, and I abide in you,
    Whatever you ask for will be done for you.

    If by your lives truly you would give God glory,
    become my disciples and keep my command.
    This is my commandment to all my disciples,
    love you one another as you I have loved.
    Greater love has no one than shown us by Jesus,
    who laid down his life so that others might live.
    This have I said to you, let me abide in you,
    that my joy remain and that your joy be full.

                       -based on John 15:1-17

    Composed by Darrin W. Snyder Belousek,
    For the ordination of Paula Snyder Belousek,
    Prairie Street Mennonite Church (2007).
    To be sung to the tune of Ash Grove (*Hymnal: A Worship Book* 478).
    Used with permission.

2. "He came down that we may have joy" (note v. 11 on *joy!*). Sing it three times for each motif, *life, light, love, peace, joy*—key emphases occurring in John 3, 8, 13, 14, 15, the order in John's Gospel.

Art
Figure 9a: *"I am the Vine you are the branches"*

Design by Jacky Briggs. © The Printery House
Conception Abbey, Conception, MO. USA. Used with permission.

Two important themes of John 15 are depicted in these two art figures.
In this image the branch draws life from the vine and bears fruit.

Figure 9b: Abide in My Love

Libby Swartley, Christmas 2012. Used with permission.

This free-hand drawn image, oil on paper, voices the heart of Jesus' Farewell, the heart of John 15, and of the Gospel as a whole.

John 16:5-33

The Work of the Paraclete;

Jesus' Departure and Consolation: Joy and Peace

Nuggets

Jesus now prepares his disciples more urgently for his departure, saying, "I will not leave you orphaned." In the first part (vv.5-15) Jesus' instructs them a fourth and fifth time on the Paraclete: what the Advocate/Spirit of truth will do for them in his absence.

Jesus informs them of coming events with two motifs: "no see/see again" and *a little while* riddle. The disciples are puzzled. Human emotions rise to the surface. Jesus guides their thought and emotions through the stages of their groping.

Acknowledging their *hearts of sorrow*, Jesus introduces new imagery: a woman going through the pain of child-birth and then rejoicing when the baby is born. Jesus uses feminine, maternal imagery to explain to his male disciples the crisis they will soon face. While the pain and joy in v. 21 may refer to Jesus himself, in vv. 22-23 Jesus uses these images for the disciples. First they will experience pain, and then later joy. Jesus promises peace.

Meditation

1. Exposition on the Paraclete *passages* is sparse in Anabaptism. A good morning and evening prayer resource that highlights the Spirit's role in Scripture (OT and NT) is the two weeks of Pentecost readings in *Take our Moments and our Days: An Anabaptist Prayer Book*, Vol. 2: *Advent Through Pentecost*, 685-890. Another resource that aids this deficiency is Kropf and Hall's *Praying with the Anabaptists*.

2. Look through your favorite hymnal(s) and note the hymns on the Holy Spirit. Identify your favorites and sing or play them (with musical instrument). Listen to your favorite Holy Spirit hymns on CD or other mode. Do any of these hymns mention the *Paraclete* as such?

3. Identify in the hymns you've selected the *Paraclete* emphases in John 14-16:
    - The *abiding* presence of Jesus
    - Witness/testify to Jesus
    - Teach you/us and remind you/us of Jesus' words
    - Comfort you/us in distress
    - Guide you/us into truth
    - *Advocate* on our behalf (or mediate your needs to Jesus or God)
    - Reprove/convict the world of sin, righteousness, and judgment
    - Declare to you the things that are to come

Try incorporating some of these *Paraclete* emphases into your own creative gift in a poem or hymn lyric.

Song

1. One of my favorite hymns is "Loving Spirit" (*Sing the Journey* 34, text by Shirley Erena Murray [1987]). Stanza 4 stresses comfort, but does not express the full range of meaning in the *Paraclete*. So I write another stanza:

    Loving Spirit, you who teach us, guide us into Jesus' truth;
    You support, cheer, and defend us from our foes and this world's hate.

For a Response of Affirmation, sing: "Don't be afraid" (*Sing the Journey* 105).

2. A marvelous hymn is "*May Thy Blessed Spirit*" by P. Tschenokoff, Arr. F. B. Cookson, sung by the Sarasota Mennonite Male Voice choir at its 2011 Festival under the direction of Lloyd Kauffman. The hymn opens our human spirit to the Holy Spirit. Think of hymns or poems that do the same for you.

Art
Figure 10: Peace on Earth

Peace on Earth—golds, greens, reds; original design.
Description: size 47 x 60. Made with "cotton fabrics, hand-quilted."
© Shirley A. Shenk (Quilt Designs, Goshen, Indiana).
Used with permission

Read John 14:27 and 16:33, and then 20:19-22. Peace is important in John's Gospel. The dove is a symbol of peace, as in the art fabric design by Shirley A. Shenk. For the dove descending and *remaining/abiding* (form of *menō*) on Jesus, see 1:32. John's use of *abiding* in 1:32 (also in 4:40, NRSV "stayed," and 10:40, NRSV, "remained") anticipates John 15, *abiding in Jesus* as branches to a vine in order to bear fruit. John's peace emphases are promises to believers, but the mission "Commission" in 20:22, framed by "Peace be with you," paves the way for Luke's "Peace on Earth" in 2:14. What symbolism do you see in this quilted wall-hanging? Might the beautiful blending of colors correlate with Jesus' prayer for the unity of all who come to believe?

John 17:1-26

Jesus Prays to His Father

Nuggets
It is not clear in John where Jesus is when he prays this prayer to his Father. This is known as Jesus' High Priestly Prayer. He is not likely in the room with his disciples, and has not yet gone with his disciples into a garden (18:1).

The prayer begins with mutual glorification: Father of Son, and Son of Father. It follows directly from Jesus' gift of peace to his disciples in 16:33. Jesus implores the Father for the protection (vv. 11-16), sanctity in truth (vv. 17-19) and, climactically, the unity of the believers.

The progression of Jesus' high priestly prayer moves along the axis of love:

- How much You, Father, love me and seek my glorification.
- How much I, Jesus, love You, Father, and seek to glorify You.
- How much we, Father and Son, love the disciples who have believed in the name of Jesus, and are entering into the intimacy of our mutual indwelling of love, unity, and communion, through which our word and works are one.

John 17 may be viewed as four strophes, each beginning with an imperative in Greek: glorify, vv.1 and 5; protect/keep, v.11b; and sanctify, v.17. Each imperative is followed by a historical reflection, followed by Jesus' petitions in the present tense (credit to Lois Siemens, a 2004 AMBS student). The first two sections accentuate *glory*, which recurs toward the end of the chapter as the goal and beauty of the church's unity. For the complete outline, see Web on chapter 17: http://www.heraldpress.com/bcbc/john.

Meditation

1. Often in my meditation on biblical verses, especially Philippians 2:5-
   11 or the Lord's Prayer, some praise song on the theme of *glory* will
   well up from within, such as the following:
   > Glorify your name, Lord, God the Father,
   > Glorify your name, Lord, God the Son,
   > Glorify your name, Lord, God the Spirit
   > Glorify your name in all the earth.

Meditate on these lines, and perhaps a musical tune will emerge to sing
them, as it has for me on several occasions, with variations.

2. The poignancy of the prayer's spiritual depth shines in Jean Vanier's
   flowing verse:
   > Having knelt down humbly in front of each disciple
   > to wash their feet,
   > having revealed their journey
   > and the journey of the Church,
   > through pain and joy
   > into the heart and ecstasy of God,
   > Jesus stops.
   > All has been said.
   > There is no more place for explanation or discussion.
   > It is now a moment of contemplation.
   > Jesus raises his eyes to heaven.
   > He no longer looks at the earth and at his disciples,
   > but towards the Father.
   > He is *with* the Father and *in* the Father,
   > contemplating the divine plan for creation and for humanity,
   > a plan that appears to be fulfilled
   > and becomes a song of thanksgiving.
   > And yet the plan is not fulfilled.
   > Jesus prays for its fulfillment:
   > that people may be healed of their aggressiveness,
   > hatred and fear
   > and become one,
   > one in God.
   >   (Vanier: 291)

Juxtaposing this prayer with the Prologue, Vanier sees in this prayer the completion of an all-important cycle: the Word sent by God into the world to share humanity's life now returns to his Father, with those who are Jesus' own "transformed into God."

> All is complete.
> The Word of God came from God
> and now returns to God,
> with all his friends, brothers and sisters
> in humanity united together. (292)

3. Sanctification, mission, and unity are an integrated theme in John (17:17-23):

> The sanctification of the disciples means that they belong to the Father. Jesus prays...that he would give them a place in the divine space of his fatherhood, where they can live out their new filial life, just as Jesus here on earth has sanctified himself by living out in the midst of humanity his reality as Son. (Rossé: 84)

Gerard Rossé uses the term "interiorization" to denote the disciples' "movement into the divine space that is the bosom of the Father, the place where Jesus himself lives his filial relationship" (85). But this is neither retreat from the world nor individualistic mysticism or spirituality. It is rather a corporate communion with and in the Father, and the basis for their sending: "Their remaining in the Son is at the very heart of their mission... The unity of the believers is seen as an indispensable condition for the conversion of the world" (85). The sequence is: sanctification, unity, and mission.

4. In John 17:11, 12, 15 Jesus prays that his disciples will be protected from the evil one. This part of a longer prayer for protection (Swartley 2006: 117) is helpful:

> Lord Jesus Christ, You are the Savior of the world;
> > by your cross and resurrection you have set us free.
> Deliver (Protect) us, Lord, from every evil;
> > and grant us peace and wholeness of life.

As you pray this prayer, you might replace *us* with *me*. This prayer is helpful in spiritual direction, counseling, and deliverance ministry. It frees from oppression, lifting burdens.

5. Jean Vanier's meditation on Jesus' prayer for unity accentuates *love*
    and *unity*, connecting us to Jesus' love, to the mutuality and unity of
    love that believers share with Jesus and his Father.

    > Unity does not come from the acceptance of exterior
    > structures or laws, dogmas or way of worship.
    > It surges up from a life that flows within us
    > and through us all together.
    > It is hearts and minds bonded together because they are
    > bonded in communion with Jesus.
    > It is a song, a celebration of thanksgiving.
    > It is a sign of the glory of God.
    > Ecumenism, then, is not to entice people to belong
    > to one particular church,
    > But to encourage all, beginning with ourselves,
    > to love Jesus more dearly
    > and to follow more fully the charter of life
    > given to us by Jesus in what is called the "beatitudes." (302)

6. Adrian van Kaam in *The Tender Farewell of Jesus* invites us into the
    intimate and reciprocal love that unites the Father, Son, and Holy
    Spirit.

    > To know you means to receive the grace of intimacy with
    > the Trinity and to witness the outpouring of God's love to
    > people around us....As we come to know God in the splendor
    > of this Trinitarian love, we begin to know how to live as an
    > adoptive child of the Trinity in daily life.
    >
    > Only in you, Lord, can we restore in the Christian
    > community the image of eternal Love. Please, let it be
    > restored...
    >
    > You...disclose the divine source of our unity: the Trinity.
    > "... Father, you are in me and I am in you." Our union with
    > another is to be achieved in that image, for it is the divine
    > archetype of Christian unity....
    >
    > You appeal...to our higher power of loving and knowing. It
    > transcends mere functional knowledge and vital feeling. You
    > then elevate this transcendent power by the gift of your Holy
    > Spirit. Typical of this unique, highest power of mutual love is
    > that understanding and love permeate one another...

Only this graced blend of spiritual love and understanding allows us to empathize with the divine uniqueness in one another. You call us to imitate in our care for others your care for the Father and the Father's care for you....

Twice in this passage you pray for our openness to the world: "So that the world may believe that it was you who sent me...May they be so perfected in unity that the world will recognize that it was you who sent me."

Stay with us, Lord, for "it is nearly evening and the day is almost over" (Lk 24:29). Let the Church you love become a community of mutual love and unity so that all people will recognize you living in our midst. (van Kaam, 56-57, 119-25).

Song

1. A song that strikes the unity theme of John 17, composed by Gerald Derstine and titled "Unity," makes the point, especially in its refrain:

> Jesus, help us live in peace,
> From our blindness set us free.
> Fill us with Your healing love,
> Help us live in unity.
>
> Words & Music by M. Gerald Derstine (JD Martin)
> © 1973 Gill 'n' Goldie Music (ASCAP).
> Used by permission

2. Another song that strikes the same theme in confessional affirmation is "The *church's* one foundation" (*HWB* 311). All five verses enunciate this truth and longing. Meditate on these lines.

Art

"The cross" on p. 119 was made by John Mishler for Belmont Mennonite Church fifteen years ago in tribute to a member who appreciated fine art and who left a sum of money for the church through her frugal living, making ends meet with the help of the church in providing housing for her and her daughters. Its blue-green (aqua) hue fits John's Gospel, combining divine glory (blue) with dying and resurrection (green) to give life eternal to all who believe.

Cross description: made from aluminum welded together as one piece, lightweight and freestanding to easily move as desired. Size: ca. 10.3 feet tall and cross-arm, 5.2 feet.

The window, with its Greek cross-form, suggests both an opened pathway to God the Father, to whom Jesus prays, and the cross the Father experiences as the Son endures the cross for the sake of "the life of the world" (John 6:51). The window may suggest also the globe, the world for which God in love gave himself and his only beloved Son (John 3:16). John's Gospel presents Jesus both glorifying the Father in the face of the cross and anguishing in prayer for his disciples, present and future.

Figure 11a: The Cross

Courtesy, Jen Shenk Photography;
John Mishler, Sculptor (Goshen, IN).

Figure 11b. Unity, for all believers

Jesus' prayer is for all to be one in him as he is one with the Father. This art has peoples' hands joined across cultures encircling the globe. Jesus prays for unity and love. As you reflect on this image, meditate on John 17:20-21, 23, 26.

> This art image comes from Ten Ten Thousand Villages: Hand Painted on Papyrus in Egypt, Jirmit Center.

A Responsive Reading

(The reader needs to pace this meditation properly, allowing an appropriate pause between each of the five sections).

Jesus' Prayer for His Disciples

Leader: Jesus prayed: Holy Father, keep those you have given me true to your name.

ALL: LORD JESUS, ARE OUR INTENTIONS, OUR ACTIONS TRUE TO YOUR NAME? LORD, MAKE US TRUE. (pause)

Leader: May they be one, Father, as we are one.

ALL: LORD, ARE WE REALLY ONE IN YOUR SPIRIT? HEAL OUR DIVISIONS. SHOW US HOW TO BE ONE. (pause)

Leader: Father, the world hates them because they do not belong to the world.

ALL: LORD, ARE WE CONFRONTING THE WORLD'S VALUES, ITS SEDUCTIONS? GIVE US COURAGE. KEEP OUR EYES FIXED ON YOU WE BELONG TO YOU NOT TO THE WORLD. (pause)

Leader: Make them holy, Father, in the truth. Your Word is truth.

ALL: LORD JESUS, YOU ARE THE WAY, THE TRUTH, THE LIFE. (pause)

Leader: May they be so completely one that the world will realize that it is you who has sent me. May the world realize that I have loved them as much as you have loved me.

ALL: LORD GOD, REMIND US EVERY DAY THAT YOU SENT YOUR SON, NOT TO CONDEMN THE WORLD, BUT THAT THROUGH HIM THE WORLD MIGHT BE SAVED.

The reading above creates the effect of our listening to Jesus praying. Sentence by sentence, we reflect upon each petition. The natural response is to examine our lives, and to resolve to adhere to Jesus' desire for us.

How beneficial it is for us to hear and repeat Jesus'…deepest concern— that his disciples might have unity among themselves. Jesus knew…that dissension works devastation on even the most eloquent verbal witness to the Father's saving love for the world.

-Eleanor Kreider, *Enter His Gates*, 194.

Spiritual Reflection

Lord Jesus,
    Thank you for your prayer for me
        to be protected from the evil one
            and the power(s) of the world
        so that I might be one with
            my brothers and sisters in love

As the Father was in you,
    so I desire that you, Jesus,
    be in me.
    I in you, you in me.

Make me holy by your Word, which is Truth.
    Fill me with your love, *agapē* love,
        empower me to do the works of righteousness.
            Do not forsake me, but send your Spirit
                as Counselor, Advocate,
                    Helper, Comforter.

Give to me your peace,
    not as the world gives,
        but a lasting, soothing peace
            that brings joy and courage.

Thank you for conquering the evil one.
    Free me from sin and its power,
        lead me in your way
            the Way to the Father.

You are the Way, the Truth and the Life.

            Love (*agapē?*),

            Willard

John 18:1-27

Jesus' Arrest and Jewish Trial

Peter's Denials

Nuggets

Jesus and his disciples enter a garden across the Kidron valley, where Jesus is arrested. Jesus takes the initiative, asking the approaching soldiers, "whom are you looking for?" (vv. 5 and 7). The soldiers say, "Jesus of Nazareth," Jesus' responds, "I am he," which in Greek is also I AM, the divine Tetragrammaton of Exodus 3:13-15. This shocks the soldiers; they fall backward.

Jesus is taken to the high priests, Annas and Caiaphas (vv.15-27). During this time the beloved disciple enters into the high priests' courtyard, while Peter stays outside. He denies Jesus (vv.17-18). This occurs two more times in vv. 25-27.

An interchange occurs between Jesus' uneventful Jewish trials—in sharp contrast to his trial before Pilate—and Peter's denials, as follows:

> a 18:12-14   Jesus appears before Annas, fulfilling
>   Caiaphas's prophecy
>   b 18:15-18: Peter denies Jesus
> a' 18:19-24   Jesus is "tried" before Annas, who sends him to
>   Caiaphas
>   b' 18:25-27: Peter denies Jesus a second and third time

Meditation

Peter followed Jesus three years, making an "ultimate pledge" (13:36-38). What happens to him now? Jean Vanier queries in two poetic responses:

Peter's Denial

> What Has Happened to Peter?
> He has followed Jesus for nearly three years,
> Seen the miracles, witnessed his healing love.
> Peter...now says he is not a disciple of Jesus,
> does not even know Jesus!
> Is he afraid of being arrested by the troops?

Or is it something deeper than fear?
Maybe he is going through a kind of breakdown.
He had left everything to follow Jesus
and given his whole life to be with him. (310)

Now Jesus has lost all power,
He is bound in ropes, dragged away, to be tried like a criminal.
He accepts to be powerless.
Silent, he refuses to speak or defend himself!
Why doesn't he defend himself?
Peter cannot stand it.
How can the Messiah be weak?
Peter feels cheated, angry, and upset.
He is plunged into a terrible disappointment and feelings of despair.
He could not accept Jesus, powerless, washing his feet.
He does not want to be a disciple of this weak Jesus, a weak Messiah!
He is not just denying Jesus
but denying all that he has seen, heard, and lived
during those years with him.
He is denying his own self and his own experience!
That is why he has lost his identity.

From the ideal to reality

Each of us risks being cut off from reality,
imprisoned in our own certitudes,
an ideal that we invent for ourselves
and that we cling to for security,
anything that will assure us of our worthiness
and prevent us from recognizing
our brokenness and hypocrisy. (311)

John 18:28–19:42

Jesus' Trial before Pilate

Death, and Burial

Nuggets

Each of the three events in this title is quite distinctive in John. The trial before Pilate is longer and more politically loaded than in the Synoptics. Pilate and Jesus clash over life-and-death issues: kingship, kingdom, and truth. Pilate's shrewd maneuvering of the situation traps the Jews: they confess Caesar to be their King, denying their covenant oath that Yahweh alone is their King!

The artful narrative is spiced with irony. It has seven movements, alternating between *outside* and *inside*:

A 18:28-32 Accusation: Pilate and the Jews (*Outside*)

   B 18:33-38a Testimony: Pilate and Jesus on Kingship (*Inside*)

      C 18:38b-40 Verdict: Pilate pronounces Jesus innocent (*Outside*)

         D 19:1-3 Pilate scourges Jesus;

            soldiers mock him as King (*Inside*)

      C' 19:4-8 The Verdict: Pilate pronounces Jesus innocent (*Outside*)

   B' 19:9-12 The Testimony: Pilate and Jesus on Authority (*Inside*)

A' 19:13-15a The Sentence: Pilate and the Jews and Jesus (*Outside*)

      Epilogue 19:15b-22: The Written Testimony-Inscription

Jesus' three words from the cross are distinctive to John:

- To his mother and the beloved disciple—be "mother/son" for each other
- *I thirst*
- *It is finished*

John's account of Jesus' burial is also distinctive: *Nicodemus* reappears with expensive spices to anoint Jesus, and assists Joseph of Arimathea to bury Jesus.

Meditation

1. When Jesus on the cross says, "*I thirst*," I wonder if this is a cry to unite with God. In Psalm 63 and Isaiah 55 *thirst for God* signifies desire to be close to God, to be filled with God's divine presence. In light of John's theme, "my Father's house," it may mean "I desire to return to my Father." It also attests to his humanity, and his realism

of his imminent death, which he anticipated already in 3:14, in the image of "lifted up," anticipating his giving his flesh for the life of the world (6:51). In his death, blood and water flow from his pierced side (19:34). Jesus entreats his disciples to *eat his flesh* and *drink his blood* (6:53-58). *Feasting* on Jesus' self-donation for us lies at the heart of John's Gospel. Meditate on how these images interrelate: *I thirst; my Father's house; I am the bread of life; eat my flesh and drink my blood; abide in me and I in you; blood and water from Jesus' side.* Think on these things during your next Communion service.

2. Jesus' death in John is first introduced by John the Witness saying, "*Behold, the Lamb of God who takes away the sin of the world!*" One of Richard Rohr's 2010 Lenten reflections builds on John's image of the Lamb who in his life and death takes away the sin of the world. It utilizes René Girard's analysis that Jesus' death both demonstrates and answers the scapegoat tradition. He is sacrificed by the violence of the world to restore societal peace and order. His "once-for-all" sacrifice ends scapegoat sacrifices (Heb 7:27; 9:12, 25, 28; 10:2, 10-12).

Am I more concerned about changing others or myself?

Jesus "took away the sin of the world" (John 1:29) by exposing it first of all as different than we imagined, and letting us know that our pattern of *ignorant killing,* attacking and blaming others, is in fact history's primary illusion and its primary lie. He both *revealed and resolved* the issue on the cross, so it must have been an absolutely central issue for human history and salvation.

Then Jesus invited us into a Great Participative Love, which would make it possible for us also not to hate. The game was over after Jesus, at least for those who "gazed" long enough on "the one that they had pierced" (John 19:37). For those who did not gaze, the game continued under even better disguises.

Through Jesus, we all have to face the embarrassing truth that *we ourselves* are our primary problem. It is *we* who must die, he teaches, not others! Our greatest temptation is to try to change other people instead of ourselves. Jesus allowed *himself* to be

transformed and *thus* transformed others. That is the meaning of
the necessary death of Jesus.

> (Rohr: "richard's daily meditations" [with portrait, "The
> Scapegoat" by William Holman Hunt, 1855]).

3. Pilate's inscription on the cross in Latin (*Iesus Nazarenus Rex
   Iudaeorum*) is the basis of the Christian art acronym: INRI, the first
   Greek letter of each word of this inscription. What does it mean for
   Pilate to proclaim in the three dominant languages of the time,
   "*Jesus of Nazareth, the King of the Jews*." Reflect on the irony. Is
   Pilate unwittingly answering his question, "*What is truth?*" (18:38)?
   Does he grasp the nature of Jesus' kingship (18:36)?

Song

1. On Good Friday 2010, I attended two community services, one by
   nine Mennonite churches in Elkhart (Ind.) in the AMBS chapel, and
   another at Faith Mission (Elkhart)—interdenominational for sure,
   and homeless singers. The part that stirred me most deeply was the
   unfamiliar, a Faith Mission African American choir singing in
   energetic crescendo gospel rap style the line "That's Love / He hung
   His head / for Me." While most songs voice truth descriptively, this
   song, with great feeling, put it personally. I felt God's and Jesus'
   goodness and love in that awful Friday event.

2. St. John's Passion, by J. S. Bach, is a moving passion cantata.
   Following John's Gospel text, it presents the drama of Pilate's
   interrogation of Jesus, and vice versa. The words from the cross,
   distinctive to John, accent Jesus' humanity. In "O sacred Head,
   now wounded," often sung in churches on Maundy Thursday
   or Good Friday, we hear mocking of Jesus' glory:

   > O sacred Head, now wounded,
   > with grief and shame weighed down,
   > now scornfully surrounded with thorns thine only crown!
   > O sacred Head, what glory, what bliss till now was thine!
   > Yet, though despised and gory, I joy to call thee mine.
   > (*Hymnal: A Worship Book* 252, stanza 1)

The African American spiritual, "Were you there," draws us into the gory event of glory. Each of the four verses below asks us to identify with one aspect of the sad experience. Stanza 3 is a John special:

1. Were you there when they crucified my Lord?
2. Were you there when they nailed him to the tree?
3. Were you there when they pierced him in the side?
4. Were you there when they laid him in the tomb?

Refrain: Oh! Sometimes it causes me to tremble, tremble, tremble.
Were you there when they crucified my Lord?
(*Hymnal: A Worship Book*, 257)

Numerous hymns express various aspects of the Passion event. Look in the hymn books you use, and find those precious to you. The line that caught my attention is the third stanza of "Go to dark Gethsemane" (*Hymnal: A Worship Book*, 240): "God's own sacrifice complete. 'It is finished!' hear the cry..." a distinctive emphasis in John.

Gather a group at your home next Passion season and sing together some of these hymns. Select one of the readings in the "Holy Week" section from *Take Our Moments and Our Days: An Anabaptist Prayer Book* (Vol. 2). As you read and pray, intersperse your favorite passion hymns into the reading.

128

Passion Art

At our local public library I found over a dozen Christian art books, with many portrayals of Jesus' crucifixion. One book, titled *Crucifixion*, had over a hundred portrayals of Jesus' face during his passion. The portrait that connected to me was Jan Mostaert's 1520s "Christ As Man of Sorrow" (in Finaldi's *The Image of Christ*: 118-19). Jesus' hands are bound, large tears dot his cheeks, and his face conveys deep sorrow, love, and agony. It spoke to me, "Has it come to this?"

Another more modern meaningful depiction was Jesus' thorn-crowned head titled "Mexican," in Bainton's *Behold the Christ* (154, Fig. 170). Three in Wheeler's *His Face* were realistic and moving: Anthony Van Dyck's "The Mocking of Christ" (79), Gian Francesco de Maineri's "Christ Carrying the Cross" (82), and Marco Palmezzano's "Jesus Carrying the Cross" (84). Salvador Dali's 1950-51 painting of "Christ on the Cross," with Jesus suspended above the earth and from the cross bowing over the world is most remarkable (Finaldi: cover and 200-201: also in Mary Grubb's *The Life of Christ in Art*: 117).

A striking classic is Mathis Grünewald's depiction with its INRI acronym above the cross, "The Crucifixion" from the Isenheim Alterpiece, 1510-11 (MacGregor and Langmuir: 135). Hans-Ruedi Weber *On a Friday Noon: Meditations under the Cross* combines diverse-type crucifixes with select meditations. Find a collection of art books, spend time surveying, and choose one or several and contemplate how it connects you to Jesus on the cross.

You may have seen the movie, "The Passion" by Mel Gibson. Compared to John's Gospel account, which reports the horrific act of crucifixion with one verse (19:18), the movie presents a long, suffering agony. From accounts I read (John Meacham in *Newsweek*, Feb. 16, 2004; David Neff in *ChrToday*, March 2004; and Russell Hittinger and Elizabeth Lev in *First Things* 141, March 2004:7-9) several theological issues emerge as well: the depiction of the role of the Jews and Mary's role. The extended brutal torture of Jesus exaggerates what John's Gospel tells us.

John's crucial theological features are: the title on the cross, Jesus' last words including mutual care of his mother and the Beloved Disciple for one another, Jesus' dying, and the soldier's spear piercing Jesus' side. These carry theological, political, and ecclesial significance in John. I viewed the film production, *Gospel of John*, narrated by Christopher Plummer (www.GospelofJohntheFilm.com). This follows John's text and enables one to truly hear John's distinctive account of Jesus' Passion. Journal your thoughts and feelings as you contemplate the crucifixion, with both your left and right brain responses.

John 20:1-31

Risen Jesus Ignites Mission and Community

Nuggets

Most of John 20 is distinctive to John's Gospel. In John we learn of Jesus' appearance to Mary Magdalene alone, with conversation between the two. Only in John are we told of Peter's and the Beloved Disciple's "race" to the tomb (cf. Luke 24:12). Jesus' appearance to his disciples in a locked room on two successive Sundays is also unique to John, as well as the content of his "Great Commission" to the disciples (vv. 19-23) and Thomas' encounter with Jesus.

Noteworthy events and words are:

- The Beloved Disciple is the first to believe; Peter's response is unclear.
- Mary Magdalene confesses and proclaims, *"I have seen the Lord."*
- Jesus breathes the Holy Spirit into the disciples
- The double (triple, a week later) *"Peace be with you"* combined with *so I send you* links peace and mission.
- Thomas, after seeing the risen Jesus, confesses, *"My Lord and my God!"*
- John's purpose statement is: that you might believe *Jesus is the Messiah, the Son of God, and through believing you may have life in his name.*

Poetry

Easter

Just when I thought
    there would be no light
        in the Jerusalem sky,
The Bright and Morning Star
    appeared
        and the darkness has not overcome it.

(Weems 1992: 89; used with permission)

Meditation

1. **Holy Week**
   Easter Monday
   He breathed on them

> *When it was evening on that day, the first day of the week, and the doors of the house where the disciples had met were locked for fear of the Jews,*
> *Jesus came and stood among them and said, "Peace be with you."*
> *After he said this, he showed them his hands and his side.*
> *Then the disciples rejoiced when they saw the Lord. Jesus said to them again,*
> *"Peace be with you. As the Father has sent me, so I send you."*
> *When he had said this, he breathed on them and said to them,*
> *"Receive the Holy Spirit.*
> *If you forgive the sins of any, they are forgiven them;*
> *if you retain the sins of any, they are retained."*
> John 20:19-23 (NRSV)

Alleluia! Christ is Risen!

*****

I have often wondered what it would have been like to have been hiding in that room with all those questions running through my mind. The apostles were so weak, so human, just like me. That's why I have always related to them. Each of them had committed themselves to following Jesus, and at the first sign of trouble, they fled from him. That, it seems to me, is a basic definition of sin: Not trusting in God when things get difficult. And so it seems totally appropriate to me that upon first entering through the locked door into that hiding place, the resurrected Jesus would address his disciples with a greeting of peace. With that simple "peace be with you" Jesus did so much for those very ordinary men: he forgave them. And in forgiving them he empowered them to be sent out to proclaim the Good News to all the world, just as the Father had sent Jesus to do the same. He empowered them to be workers for peace.

Then Jesus "breathes on them" and with this very intimate act, something he has done in other places when raising the dead or healing the sick, he communicates a kind of unity with all humanity. He tells his disciples that they are to "receive the Holy Spirit" by his breath. You see, we are united in the breath that is the Holy Spirit. This was more obvious to those who could read John's Gospel in the original Greek, for breath and spirit are the same word in that language. That breath is shared with all humanity.

Finally he instructs them, "If you forgive the sins of any, they are forgiven them; if you retain the sins of any, they are retained." In some circles within Christianity, that passage has been interpreted as one only applicable to those who are ordained. I have never read it that way. When I read this passage, I hear Jesus telling us one more time that we are united with one another, and with him in such a way that if we act to free our sisters and brothers from whatever it is that binds them to the sin and death and hell that they have brought upon themselves and others, then we are all free. If we insist on keeping our sisters and brothers chained to that same sin and death and hell, then they are chained, but so are we. If one is choking for lack of breath, we all suffocate.

So whether we are forgiving those who have harmed us, threatened us, or wished evil upon us; or if we are seeking forgiveness from those whom we have harmed, threatened, or wished evil upon, we are engaging in the creation of peace. We have the tools for peace within our reach. Jesus taught that to us in so many different ways, and the most basic tool he used was forgiveness. Whether we need to grant forgiveness or seek forgiveness from the neighbor who lives in our own home, down the street, or in another country, we have been given all we need to eventually live in a peaceful way. If we are to achieve peace before the sun goes down, we must first begin with forgiveness. This Eastertide, I invite you to allow Jesus to breathe on you and receive his greeting of peace. Then spread that breath around.

The Lord is risen indeed!

Alleluia!

Brother James Dowd, *Seasoned with Peace: Spring* (2011: 105-7) Compiled by Susan Mark Landis (used with permission).

2. John 20:19-23 integrates Peace, Mission, and Forgiveness. Jesus appears to his disciples, greeting them with "Peace be with you" three times (19, 21, 26). As Jesus breathes the Holy Spirit upon/into his disciples he encircles them with peace, commissions them to mission, and grants them authority to forgive sins. We may think "forgiveness of sins" is what Catholic priests do for Catholics in "confession." But this text says "forgiveness of sins" lies at the heart of Christian mission and peacemaking. True, it is not something *we* can do out of our own goodness or righteousness. Rather, it is the gospel we proclaim and bear witness to in our lives. We speak words of forgiveness in the name of Jesus Christ. If the gospel is not proclaimed, then sins are retained. The good news of the gospel is that through it we can lead people to forgiveness and peace. Baptism publicly witnesses to receiving by God's grace these blessed gifts of Jesus Christ: the gospel of peace with commission to mission and to forgive sins. This is both a personal and corporate calling. How well do we do it?

3. Menno Simons bears witness to a heart saturated with peace and mission. God sent Jesus to proclaim gospel of peace. What a heart-interweaving of peace-Scriptures!

> Do consider how you together with all Christians are received and called by the God of peace, under the Prince of Peace, by the messengers of peace, to the body of peace, with the Word of peace, into the kingdom of peace, out of mere love and grace.
>
> Therefore walk in that same peace, so that in that day you may in His grace be able to stand before your God with a confident and happy conscience when body and soul must part.
>
> The Lord of peace grant you His peace in all places and in every manner.
>
> May that selfsame peace keep your hearts and minds in Christ Jesus. Amen!
>
> Menno, to the beloved brothers and sisters in Christ
> in Prussia, October 7, 1549 (in Wenger, ed: 1034-35).

Song

"The risen Christ, who walks on wounded feet" (*Sing the Story* 101), with lyrics by Nigel Weaver (and music by Joseph Funk, 1832), describes the risen Jesus as coming to his disciples and speaking the word of peace (stanza 1) and then breathing out his Spirit on them to give new grace, strength and purpose. Find the hymn if you have access to the song book, and meditate on all its stanzas.

Holy Spirit, truth divine
Holy Spirit, Truth divine, dawn upon this soul of mine.
 Voice of God, and inward Light, wake my spirit, clear my sight.
Holy Spirit, Love divine, glow within this heart of mine.
 Kindle ev'ry high desire, purify me with your fire.
Holy Spirit, Power divine, fill and nerve this will of mine.
 Boldly may I always live, bravely serve and gladly give.
Holy Spirit, Peace divine, still this restless heart of mine.
 Speak to calm this tossing sea, grant me your tranquility.
Holy Spirit, Joy divine, gladden now this heart of mine.
 In the desert ways I sing, spring, O living Water, spring!
 Stanzas 1, 2 , 3, 5, 6. Text, Samuel Longfellow. *Hymnal: A Worship Book* 508

Art
Figure 12: "Resurrection" Batik

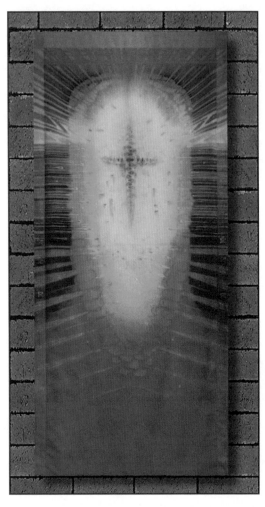

This art image in the Holy Trinity Church reflects the light of Jesus' resurrection radiating from the cross in all directions and dimensions through multi-color toning.

Batiked hanging-cloth by **Gwen Jackson** (used with permission)
Holy Trinity Church, Exmouth, Devon, U.K.
Photograph by Leo Spillane

Figure 13: Mary Magdalene and the Risen Jesus

For citation of artistic depictions of Mary Magdalene as she meets Jesus, see M. Edwards: 195. In Renaissance paintings Jesus' response to Mary to not touch (KJV) or hold on to me (NRSV) shows in different ways vacillation in Mary's posture and in Jesus' as well:

From 2belife.blogspot.com, posted April 2010 (original source unknown)

Imagine the trauma Mary Magdalene experiences seeking to see and comprehend the risen Jesus, the Jesus she deeply loves. Trauma overloads the human senses and spirit, often skewing the memory and ability to state clearly what happened. What in your own life-experience approximates such sudden shift in mood of experience? How have you coped with it?

Figure 14: Thomas Encounters Jesus

Albrecht Dürer (1471-1528)
Woodcut: 5 x 3.3 inches

Thomas, often known as the "doubter," seeks evidence for such a wild claim: Jesus is risen from the dead. When he sees Jesus he does not need to touch, but exclaims, "*My Lord, and my God!*" This is truly the climax to John's Gospel's Christology, harking back to John 1:1 and Jesus' seven absolute *I AM* claims, evoking God's self-revelation to Moses (Exod 3:13-15).

Thomas exclaims, "*My Lord, and my God!*" This Woodcut by Albrecht Dürer (1471-1528), accentuates Thomas's touching Jesus' side wound.

For more art images of Thomas, go to Google, select Image, and search for "Jesus and Thomas in the Bible." Identify two or three images that are meaningful to you. Then meditate on the following comments (see my commentary, *John*, pp. 463-55, for fuller narrative).

Jesus meets Thomas on the terms Thomas stated a week earlier: *Put your finger here and see my hands. Reach out your hand and put it in my side*. Jesus continues: *Do not doubt but believe*. Thomas has been viewed by commentators as "doubting Thomas," most common; as "stubborn Thomas" because he refuses to believe; or as "sincere Thomas" in his quest for evidence to believe.

Whichever view we take, Thomas's confession functions in John's Gospel as the matching bookend to what the Gospel says in 1:1: *The Word was God*. Thomas's confession has important canonical and political significance. *Lord* (*kyrios*) is the standard translation of the sacred name revealed to Moses in Exodus 3:13-15: *I AM who I AM*. Thus on the one hand this climactic confession reveals Jesus' true identity as *YHWH*-Lord and *Elohim*-God. Emperor Domitian, during whose reign this Gospel was likely written, also claimed this title: *Dominus et Deus noster* (our Lord and God, in Latin). Thomas's confession, on the other hand, repudiates the emperor's claim. Not Domitian, but Jesus is the true Lord and God.

Thomas's confession testifies to Thomas's belief and obedience, converting his worldview and relationship to Jesus. It also prefigures Thomas's future role as apostolic witness. The Mar Thoma churches of Syria and India regard Thomas as their founding apostle.

Jesus meets Thomas where he is. Our response to Jesus may merge with his, confessing Jesus as our Lord and God incarnate.

John 21:1-25

New Horizons and Destinies

Nuggets

With this chapter we shift north to Galilee (recall Jesus' leaving Galilee way back in chapter 7). The characters in this chapter are Jesus and seven disciples: *Simon Peter, Thomas called the Twin, Nathanael of Cana in Galilee, the sons of Zebedee, and two others of his disciples* (v. 2). Who are these others? Likely one is the Beloved Disciple, unless that person is one of the unnamed sons of Zebedee.

Jesus reunites with this select group of disciples after their failed and then blessed fishing episode and, most importantly, around a charcoal fire, the *second time* for Simon Peter! This is the context for Jesus' *"Do you love me?"* quiz he gives to Peter (vv. 15-17).

The final episode is Jesus' prophecy of Peter's future and call, *"Follow me,"* linked to the mystery of the Beloved Disciple's identity and future. Key to this is his role of eyewitness to Jesus and author or key tradition-bearer for the Gospel's content (v. 24).

Meditation

Chapter 21 is important to the Gospel for Peter's healing of memories. *Three times* Peter denied Jesus, and Jesus has appeared now to Peter *three times*. Moreover Jesus now engages him, eye to eye, extending to him *three times* the opportunity and grace to renew his love for Jesus, which Peter had ardently pledged at the last supper. Different words are used here for love.

Jesus asks for *agapē*, self-giving love, but Peter in his painful discovery of his weakness answers with *phileō*, the love of friendship. Even though in other places in John's Gospel no significant distinction is evident, the different verbs here appear intentional and significant. When the gap between self-giving love and friendship love is not closed in Simon's second response, Jesus shifts to friendship love in his third question. That contributes to the sting of Peter's hurt in being asked the third time, *"Do you love me?"*

141

Nonetheless, Peter says *yes three times* and *three times* Jesus commissions him to a leadership role in the church, *Feed my lambs* first, then feed *my sheep*, then feed *my little sheep.* This emotionally filled interchange between Jesus and Peter is God bestowing grace to Peter, allowing those horrible memories of his denial *standing by the fire* to be replaced by *another later standing by the fire* at this seaside breakfast to renew his love.

Jesus calls him finally and firmly to the Peter/rock position he will have among Jesus' followers. Jesus then prophesies Peter's future: Peter will faithfully follow him (Jesus) even unto death (21:19).

Drama

Jesus' dialogue-encounter with Simon Peter (arranged by author)
(Readers theatre for three: narrator, Jesus, and Peter)

Narrator: When they had finished breakfast, Jesus said to Simon Peter,

> **Jesus**: *"Simon son of John, do you love me more than these?"*

Narrator: He said to him,

> **Simon**: *"Yes, Lord; you know that I love you."*

Narrator: Jesus said to him,

> **Jesus**: *"Feed my lambs."*

Narrator: A second time he said to him,

> **Jesus**: *"Simon son of John, do you love me?"*

Narrator: He said to him,

> **Simon**: *"Yes, Lord; you know that I love you."*

Narrator: Jesus said to him,

> **Jesus**: "Tend my sheep."

Narrator: He said to him the third time,

> **Jesus**: *"Simon son of John, do you love me?"*

Narrator: Peter felt hurt because he said to him *the third time,*
> "Do you love me?"
> And he said to him,

> **Simon**: "Lord, you know everything; you know that I love you."

Narrator: Jesus said to him,

> **Jesus**: *"Feed my sheep."*

Sermon on Peter
"Standing by the Fire; Healing the Memories"
Willard Swartley (Belmont Neighborhood Fellowship, 2010)

When the famed New York Giants played in the 1912 World Series, Fred Snodgrass, in the tenth inning with tied score, made a costly error. A fly ball fell into his mitt, but he dropped it. Sixty-two years later, when he died at age 86, the *New York Times* obituary read: "Fred Snodgrass, 86, Dead: Ball Player Muffed 1912 Fly."

In the Gospels, especially in John, Peter is a Fred Snodgrass. At the crucial moment he dropped the ball in following Jesus. He had trained and was determined not to do so. He aspired to be Jesus' right-hand, dependable support, but when the chips were down, he flubbed.

We look briefly at seven scenes in Peter's life.

Scene 1. South of the Sea of Galilee, east of the Jordan River. In John 1:40-42, Andrew, one of Jesus' first disciples, finds his brother Peter, and says to him, *"We have found the Messiah."* Andrew then takes Peter to meet Jesus. Jesus looks at him and says, *"You are Simon, son of John. You are to be called Cephas"* (*which means Peter*). That's quick; Peter gets a job and a position with a new name, on the spot, to train with Jesus the Messiah. He begins to travel with Jesus and other disciples.

Scene 2. In Capernaum. A year (or two) later, we meet Peter again, shortly after Jesus feeds five thousand hungry people and announces himself to be the bread of life. The religious leaders are upset with Jesus. But Jesus keeps teaching, somewhat in riddles, making it clear that those who would follow him will have to count the cost. Many of Jesus' disciples decided at that point to "throw in the towel." They "turn back" from following Jesus. Then Jesus (in 6:67) puts it to the twelve: "'*Do you also wish to go away?'* Simon Peter answers him, *"Lord, to whom can we go? You have the words of eternal life. We have come to believe and know that you are the Holy One of God."* Peter sticks with Jesus. Shortly after this, Jesus makes his final trip to Jerusalem. For several months we hear nothing about Peter.

Scene 3. The Last Supper (ch. 13). After dinner is finished Jesus does the unthinkable. He begins to wash the disciples' feet. Peter is horrified and protests, *"You will never wash my feet."* Jesus persists, and tells Peter

143

if he refuses he has no part with him, no sharing in what Jesus has come to do. Peter then switches his tune and asks Jesus to wash his whole body, obtuse in grasping the servant role that Jesus calls the disciples to take on. Jesus washes Peter's feet.

Later at the table Jesus speaks about one who will betray him. Peter is curious and asks the Beloved Disciple, who reclines on Jesus, to ask Jesus who will betray him. At the end of this last supper Jesus gives his disciples a new commandment, to love one another as he has loved them. Jesus has also told them he will be with them only a little longer. Peter picks up on this and asks, *"Lord, where are you going?"* Jesus answers, *"Where I am going, you cannot follow me now; but you will follow afterward."* Peter said to him, *"Lord, why can I not follow you now? I will lay down my life for you."* Jesus answers, *"Will you lay down your life for me? Very truly, I tell you, before the cock crows, you will have denied me three times."*

Scene 4. In the (Mt. Olivet?) garden. Jesus has ended his Farewell Discourse and in it (chs. 14–17) we hear nothing from Peter. But later that night when Jesus goes into the garden and a band of soldiers comes to arrest Jesus, Peter draws his sword and cuts off the ear of Malchus, the servant of the Jewish high priest. Jesus reprimands Peter and says, *"Put your sword back into its sheath. Am I not to drink the cup the Father has given me?"* (18:11).

Just a few verses and minutes later Jesus is taken into the courtyard of the Jewish high priest. The Beloved Disciple goes in with Jesus, but Peter stays outside. A woman guard at the courtyard door asks Peter, *"You are not also one of this man's disciples, are you?"* The question is framed to make it easy for Peter to respond negatively. He says, *"No, I am not."* Then he saunters over to the charcoal fire to warm himself. He mixes in with slaves and the police who arrested Jesus.

About an hour later, after the elder high priest turns Jesus over to the younger high priest, Peter is still *standing by the fire*, warming himself. Some in the circle asked him the same question, *"You are not one of his disciples, are you?"* Peter again denies he knows Jesus, saying, *"I am not."* But now a slave, a relative of the man whose ear Peter cut off, says, *"Did I not see you in the garden with him?"* Peter denies; the cock crows!

Peter leaves the area. We hear nothing of Peter during the rest of the gory story of Jesus' passion, when Pilate tries Jesus and crucifies him. Peter is in hiding.

JESUS IS CRUCIFIED AND PETER IS NOWHERE AROUND.

We can only imagine Peter's feelings: anger, self-pity, despair, remorse—just plain sick inside and all over.

Scene 5. Early Easter morning, Peter and the Beloved Disciple are awakened by an excited voice at their door. Mary Magdalene is telling them she's been to the tomb, the stone is rolled back, and they've taken away Jesus' body. As fast as possible the two run to the tomb, with the Beloved Disciple outrunning Peter. The Beloved Disciple looks in, steps back, and ushers Peter in. Peter inspects the scene: He sees "*the linen wrappings lying there, and the cloth that had been on Jesus' head, not lying with the linen wrappings but rolled up in a place by itself.*" But we hear not a word from Peter. The Beloved Disciple then enters, sees the same things Peter saw; *he saw and believed.* He always has an edge over Peter in John's Gospel. He is a special, mysterious disciple, the one whom Jesus loved, and the one who knows the heart of Jesus.

Later that evening the disciples were gathered in a room with doors locked for "*fear of 'the Jews'*" (20:19). Suddenly Jesus appears in their midst and greets them, "*Peace be with you.*" Jesus commissions them and breathes on them the Holy Spirit—that's another sermon. Peter says nothing. In ch. 20 where the risen Lord appears three times, to Mary Magdalene, to the ten, and again a week later when Thomas is with them, we never hear a word from Peter. He is too humiliated to speak among his peers. He earlier ardently pledged to follow Jesus at all costs, but he blew it.

Scene 6. Some time has elapsed and the new location is the Sea of Galilee, ninety miles north of Jerusalem. Apparently the fisher disciples decided to head home and go back to their trade. So seven of them go fishing during the night, when the fish bite and they can be alone with their thoughts in the dark. They fish all night but catch nothing, not even one. Then almost at day break they see a form of someone on the shore 100 yards away. The man calls out, "*You have no fish, have you?*" It's a strange way to ask the question. It sounds like "*You are not one of his disciples, are you?*" The disciples shout back, and say, "*No.*" Then the stranger on the beach dares to instruct these seasoned fishermen, commanding them, *"Cast the net to the right side of the boat, and you will find some."* They do so. Suddenly their net is so full of fish they can't get it overboard into the boat.

Just then the disciple, the one Jesus loved, says, *"It is the Lord!"* Simon Peter, hearing this, naked though he be, quickly puts on some clothes and jumps into the sea, slogging toward that stranger on the beach. Peter trusts the Beloved Disciple—his love *sees* and *knows*. The other disciples bring in the boat, dragging the huge net full of big fish. When they gather on the shore *"they saw a charcoal fire there, with fish on it, and some bread."* Simon Peter now *draws* the net ashore, and it's full of big fish, 153 of them—I suppose stupefied Peter counted them. The man says, *"Come, eat breakfast."* And, *all the while no one dared ask him who he was, because they all knew it was the Lord.* Then *Jesus came and took the bread and gave it to them, and did the same with the fish. This was now the third time that Jesus appeared to the disciples after he was raised from the dead.*

Scene 7. Same morning, same location, on the seashore, by the charcoal fire. After breakfast is finished, Jesus engages Simon Peter in dialogue, and addresses him, not as Peter, but as *Simon, son of John*, a flashback to their first encounter in 1:42. A searching "question and answer" session ensues. Peter's restoration and healing of memories are couched in the present and future reality of Peter's response to Jesus' piercing question: *Do you love me?*

> *"Simon son of John, do you love me more than these?" Peter said to him, "Yes, Lord; you know that I love you." Jesus said to him, "Feed my lambs."*
>
> *A second time he said to him, "Simon son of John, do you love me?" He said to him, "Yes, Lord; you know that I love you." Jesus said to him, "Tend my sheep."*
>
> *He said to him the third time, "Simon son of John, do you love me?" Peter felt hurt because he said to him the third time (3x), "Do you love me?" And he said to him, "Lord, you know everything; you know that I love you." Jesus said to him, "Feed my sheep."* (21:15-17)

This is the healing of Peter's memory. *Three times* Peter denied Jesus, and Jesus has by now appeared to Peter and the disciples *three times* since his resurrection (21:14). Moreover Jesus now engages Peter, eye to eye, extending to him *three times* the opportunity and grace to renew his love for Jesus, which Peter had ardently pledged at the Last Supper. Different words are used here for love, but John's Gospel overall doesn't seem to make a big distinction between them. Peter affirms friendship love but falters on self-giving agape love. But Peter does say *yes three times* and *three times* Jesus commissions him to a leadership role in the church, *Feed my lambs, my sheep, my sheep.* In this emotionally filled interchange between Jesus and Peter God bestows grace to Peter, replacing those horrible memories of his denials while standing by the fire with another later standing by the seaside fire to renew Peter's pledge to follow, now based on love (echo John 13:34-38). Jesus now appoints him to the Peter/rock position he will have as shepherd-leader of Jesus' followers.

Peter's journey with Jesus invites us to remember our pledges, our denials of our Lord, and need for God's forgiving grace to heal our painful memories. I invite you (if you are physically able) to journey (to the front), to the first charcoal fire, and remember, as the Lord brings it to your mind, when you in some way denied Jesus. Then I invite you to journey to the other charcoal fire, stand by it, and feel Jesus' welcome. Then move to the seashore where Jesus engaged Peter to renew his love for Jesus and commissioning him to his future life and vocation. Ask God to restore you into his love and direction. Pick up a seashell or weathered glass as a memory of your journey. Keep it where you can see it and relive that journey, as you need and want to.

You might do as I did for props for this sermon. Two charcoal pits (saucers) filled with charcoal at different locations and a sea-shore color blanket with a spread of either weathered sea glass or sea shells or both.

THE WORD   I AM
Antiphon

In the beginning was the WORD		1:1
I AM (is) speaking with you	**4:26**	
And the WORD was with God		1:1
I AM working with my Father still	**5:17**	
And the WORD was God		1:1
I AM, do not be afraid	**6:20**	
He was in the beginning with God		1:2
I AM the bread of life	**6:35**	
All things came into being through him		1:3
I AM from Him and He sent me	**7:29**	
Without him not one thing came into being		1:3
I AM with you a little while longer,		
then I go to Him who sent me	**7:33**	
In Him was life		1:4
I AM the light of the world	**8:12**	
And the life was the light of all people		1:4
I AM judging no one	**8:15**	
The light shines in the darkness		1:5
I AM not alone	**8:16**	
And the darkness did not overcome it		1:5
I AM from above	**8:23**	
The true light, which enlightens everyone,		
was coming into the world		1:9
I AM not from this world	**8:23**	
He was in the world		1:10
I AM, before Abraham was	**8:58**	
And the world came into being through him		1:10
I AM in the world	**9:5**	
Yet the world did not know him		1:10
I AM the gate for my sheep	**10:7**	
He came to his own		1:11
I AM the good shepherd	**10:11**	
And his own people did not accept him		1:11
I AM the resurrection and the life	**11:25**	

Painted on a 120g royal blue card with colored ink and "Prisma" colored pencils.

But to all who received him	1:12
I AM where my servant shall be	**12:26**
Who believed in his name	1:12
I AM Teacher and Lord	**13:13**
He gave power to become children of God	1:12
YOU ARE my disciples	**13:35**
Who were born	1:13
I AM the Way, the Truth, and the Life	**14:6**
Not of blood or the will of the flesh or the will of man	1:13
I AM in the Father and the Father is in me	**14:11**
But of God	1:13
I AM the true vine	**15:1**
And the WORD became flesh	1:14
YOU ARE my friends	**15:14**
And lived among us	1:14
I AM, be with me	**17:24**
And we have seen his glory	1:14
I AM Jesus of Nazareth	**18:5**
The glory of the Father's only Son	1:14
I AM thirsty	**19:28**
Full of grace and truth	1:14
IT IS finished	**19:30**
No one has ever seen God. It is God the only Son, who is close to the Father's heart, who has made him known.	1:18
I AM sending you, as the Father has sent me.	
Peace be with you. Follow me.	**20:21, 21:19**

Note: These are most of Jesus' I AM statements from the Gospel of John, removing repetitions. Not checked against original languages.

Jim Longley (2006 AMBS student; used with permission).

Art
Figure 15 Antiphon Calligraphy of Word / I AM
Sally Longley made this calligraphy as a gift for Jim. May its beauty attract you to John's Gospel as indeed a work of art that elicits worship in "the beauty of holiness" (Ps 96:9, KJV).

Trim Size: 820mm high x 282mm wide (30 inches long)! Used with permission.

THE WORD
I AM

In the beginning was the WORD   1:1

I AM (is) speaking with you   4:21
    And the WORD was with God   1:1

I AM working with my Father still   5:17
    And the WORD was God   1:1

I AM, do not be afraid   6:20
    He was in the beginning with God   1:2

I AM the bread of life   6:35
    All things came into being through him   1:3

I AM from Him and He sent me   7:29
    Without him not one thing came into being   1:3

I AM with you a little while longer,   7:33
then I go to Him who sent me
    In him was life   1:4

I AM the light of the world   8:12
    And the life was the light of all people   1:4

I AM judging no one   8:15
    The light shines in the darkness   1:5

I AM not alone   8:16
    And the darkness did not overcome it   1:5

I AM from above   8:23
    The true light, which enlightens everyone,
    was coming into the world   1:9

I AM not from this world   8:23
    He was in the world   1:10

I AM before Abraham was   8:58
    And the world came into being through him   1:10

I AM in the world   9:5
    Yet the world did not know him   1:10

I AM the gate for my sheep	10:7
He came to his own	1:11
I AM the good shepherd	10:11
And his own people did not accept him	1:11
I AM the resurrection and the life	11:25
But to all who received him	1:12
I AM where my servant shall be	12:26
Who believed in his name	1:12
I AM Teacher and Lord	13:13
He gave power to become children of God	1:12
YOU ARE my disciples	13:35
Who were born	1:13
I AM the Way, the Truth, and the Life	14:6
Not of blood or the will of the flesh	1:13
or the will of man	
I AM in the Father and the Father is in me	14:11
But of God	1:13
I AM the true vine	15:1
And the WORD became flesh	1:14
YOU ARE my friends	15:14
And lived among us	1:14
I AM, be with me	17:24
And we have seen his glory	1:14
I AM Jesus of Nazareth	18:5
The glory of the Father's only Son	1:14
I AM thirsty	19:28
Full of grace and truth	1:14
IT IS finished	19:30
No one has ever seen God. It is God, the	
only son, who is close to the Father's	
heart, who has made him known.	1:18
I AM sending you as the Father has sent me.	20:21
Peace be with you. Follow me.	21:19

Spiritual Reflection

Jesus, God sent You into the world as
    Light
        Life
            Love,
  and now you say
        So send I you.

Breathe into me the Holy Spirit
    to be sent
        to forgive sins
            to prevail over sins
    So that I am freed
        and enabled to help others to freedom
            from sin and the evil one's dominion

Do I love You, Lord Jesus,
    truly love you enough to follow, even
        through suffering and death for your sake?

Look upon me, give me sight, empower me
    to embody the model of the beloved disciple
        and with Peter feed your sheep.

Willard

Benediction Blessing

Two texts [from John] serve as the basis for the short phrases of this benediction. The words "do not let your heart be troubled" from the New International Version have given way to the simpler "don't be worried and upset" (TEV). Jesus' words, "I am sending you" and "receive the Spirit" are the basis for the response (ALL). But they appear in the form of a resolution to live the life of the Spirit in peace.

> *"Peace be with you! As the Father has sent me,*
> *I am sending you."*
> *And with that he breathed on them and said,*
> *"Receive the Holy Spirit"* (John 20:21-22).
> *"My peace I give you . . . Do not let your hearts be troubled*
> *and do not be afraid"* (John 14:27).

Leader: Jesus said: Peace is what I leave with you.
Don't be worried and upset.
Don't be afraid.
My own peace is what I am giving to you.

All: *Let us go out in the Spirit of Jesus. Let us go out into his peace.*

Eleanor Kreider, *Enter His Gates*, 207-208

Figure 16: "Journey" by Kris A. Shenk
Lenten Banners 2013 for Belmont Mennonite Church
Each banner: 54 inches x 144 inches; overall size: 108 inches x 144 inches.
Photo editing, Mary E. Klassen

What in this banner connects to your journey though John's Gospel? With Gospel lenses I see: "Journey" with glory-light, crosses and God's heart of love "from above."

Bibliography (sources cited)

Ackerman Link, Julie
    2011 Our Daily *Bread* (July 5).
Boers, Arthur, *et al.*
    2010 *Take Our Moments and Our Days: An Anbaptist Prayer Book*. Vol.
        1: Ordinary time; Vol. 2: *Christian Seasons: Advent through*
        Pentecost. Elkhart, IN.: IMS and Scottdale, PA: Herald Press.
Brenneman, Diane Zaerr
    2009 *Words for Worship 2*. Scottdale, PA: Herald Press.
Brodie, Thomas L.
    1993 *The Gospel According to John: A Literary and Theological*
        Commentary. Oxford: University Press.
Burge, Gary M.
    2000 *John; The NIV Application Commentary*. Grand Rapids: Zondervan.
Coloe, Mary L.
    2001 *God Dwells with Us: Temple Symbolism in the Fourth Gospel.*
        Collegeville, MN: Liturgical Press.
    2007 *Dwelling in the Household of God: Johannine Ecclesiology and*
        Spirituality. Collegeville, MN: Liturgical Press.
Dalí, Salvador, Max Gérard, and Eleanor R. Morse
    1986 *Dali*. New York: Abradale Press/H.N. Abrams.
Day, Janeth Norfleete
    2002 *The Woman at The Well: Interpretation of John 4:1-42 in Retrospect*
        And Prospect.
        Leiden: Brill.
de Waal, Esther
    2009 *Seeking Life: The Baptismal Invitation of the Rule of St. Benedict*.
        Collegeville, MN: Liturgical Press.
Dürer, Albrecht (see Kurth)
Edwards, Mark
    2004 *John*. Blackwell Bible Commentaries. Oxford and Malden, Mass.:
        Blackwell.
Ellul, Jacques
    1985 *The Humiliation of the Word*. Trans. by Joyce Main Hanks. Grand
        Rapids: Eerdmans.
Finaldi, Gabriele, Neil MacArthur, and Susanna Avery-Quash
    2000 *The Image of Christ* (National Gallery London). New Haven, CT:
        Distributed by Yale University Press.
Fox, George
    2002 *QuakerPsalms: A Book of Devotions*. Compiled and arranged by T. S.
        Wallace. Camp Hill, PA: Foundation Publications.

Freeman, Arthur
    1992 and 1983. The URL for this poetry is:
http://www.moravianseminary.edu/images/moravianseminary/ArtFreeman/Poetry/LifesM
ystery.pdf

    Other inspiring Freeman contributions are also on-line:
    http://www.moravianseminary.edu/moravian-studies/online-
    resources.html
Grün, Anselm
    2002 *Images of Jesus*. Trans. John Bowden. New York/London:
        Continuum.
Hymnal: A Worship Book (*HWB*)
    1992 Prepared by Churches in the Believers Church Tradition. Elgin, IL:
        Brethren Press; Newton, KS: Faith and Life Press; Scottdale, PA:
        Mennonite Publishing House.
Jasper, Alison
    1998 *The Shining Garment of the Text: Gendered Readings of John's
        Prologue*. JSNTSS 165. Gender, Culture, Theory 6. Sheffield:
        Sheffield Academic Press.
Hubmaier, Balthasar. In Wayne Pipkin and John H. Yoder, trans. and eds.
    1989 *Balthasar Hubmaier: Theologian of Anabaptism*. CRR 5. Scottdale,
        PA: Herald Press.
Kasper, Cardinal Walter
    2005 "Ecumenical Situation – Ecumenical Problems – Ecumenical
        Perspectives." See Lecture 2
        http://www.lehighchurches.org/doc/campbell/2005_Campbell_Lectur
        e_1.pdf.
Katongole, Emmanuel and Chris Rice
    2008 *Reconciling All Things: A Christian Vision for Justice, Peace, and
        Healing*. Downers Grove, InterVarsity Press.
Kauffman, Ivan J.
    2000 *Those Who Knew Jesus Speak*. Grand Rapids: Brazos Press.
Kreider, Eleanor
    1990 *Enter His Gates: Fitting Worship Together*. Scottdale, PA: Herald
        Press.
Kropf, Marlene and Eddy Hall
    1994 *Praying with the Anabaptists: The Secret of Bearing Fruit*. Newton,
        KS: Faith and Life Press.
Kurth, Willi, ed.
    1946 *The Complete Woodcuts of Albrecht Dürer*. New York, Bonaza
        Books.
Landis, Susan Mark, Lisa J. Amstutz, and Cindy Snider

2011 *Seasoned with Peace: Spring.* ©Susan Mark Landis (available www.Seasoned with Peace.com)

2011 *Seasoned with Peace: Fall.* ©Susan Mark Landis. (available at www.Seasoned with Peace.com)

Landis, Susan Mark, Lisa J. Amstutz, Cindy Snider, and Judith Baer Kulp

2010 *Seasoned with Peace: Winter.* ©Susan Mark Landis. (available www.Seasoned with Peace.com)

MacGregor, Neil, and Erika Langmuir

2000 *Seeing Salvation: Images of Christ in Art.* London: BBC.

Mark, Arlene, ed.

1996 *Words for Worship.* Waterloo, ON/Scottdale, PA: Herald Press.

Neuls-Bates, Carol, ed.

1996 "Hildegard of Bingen: Abbess and Composer," in *Women in Music: An Anthology of Source Readings from the Middle Ages to the Present.* Rev. ed. Boston: Northeastern University Press.

Rohr, Richard,

2010 "The Scapegoat," Lenten Meditation (Feb 24). http://by123w.bay123.mail.live.com/default.aspx?&ip=10.1.106.221&d =d1304&mf=a0)

Rossé, Gerard

2009 *Community of Believers: A New Look at the Johannine Writings.* Trans. Matthew J. O'Connell. New York: New City Press; a new edition of *The Spirituality of Communion: A New Approach to the Johannine Writings* (1998).

Schmidt, Orlando, compiler and ed.

1979 *Sing and Rejoice! New Hymns for Congregations.* Scottdale, PA/Kitchener, Ont.: Herald Press.

Sing the Journey

2005 *Hymnal: A Worship Book*; Supplement 1. Scottdale, PA: Mennonite Publishing Network; Faith and Life Division.

Sing the Story

2007 *Hymnal: A Worship Book*; Supplement 2. Scottdale, PA: Mennonite Publishing Network; Faith and Life Division.

Sink, Susan

2007 *THE ART OF THE SAINT JOHN'S BIBLE: A Reader's Guide to Pentateuch, Psalms, Gospels and Acts.* Collegeville, MN: Saint John's University, ©Order of Saint Benedict.

Snyder, C. Arnold and Galen A. Peter

2002 *Reading the Anabaptist Bible: Reflections for Every Day of the Year.* Waterloo: Pandora Press.

Swartley, Willard M.

2006 "A Prayer for Protection." In *Even the Demons Are Subject: Continuing Jesus' Ministry of Deliverance,* ed. Loren Johns and

James R. Krabill, 117. Elkhart, IN: IMS and Scottdale, PA: Herald Press.

2009 "Jesus Triumphs over the Powers," (with Michael Fecher). In *Jesus Matters: Good News for the 21st Century*. Ed. James R. Krabill and David W. Shenk, 89-103. Scottdale, PA: Herald Pr.

2012 *Health, Healing, and the Church's Mission: Biblical Perspectives and Moral Priorities*. Downers Grove: InterVarsity Press.

2013 *John*. Believers Church Bible Commentary. Harrisonburg, VA: Herald Press.

Vanier, Jean

2004 *Drawn into the Mystery of Jesus through the Gospel of John*. New York/Mahwah, NJ: Paulist Press.

Van Kaam, Adrian

1996 *The Tender Farewell of Jesus: Meditations on Chapter 17 of John's Gospel*. New York: New City Press.

Webber, Robert E.

2006 *The Divine Embrace: Recovering the Passionate Spiritual Life*. Grand Rapids: Baker.

Weems, Ann

1992 *Kneeling in Jerusalem*. Louisville, KY: Westminster/John Knox Press.

Wheeler, Maritz

1998 *His Face: Images of Christ in Art*. New York: Chameleon Books, Inc.

Witherington, Ben III

2006 "The Last Man Standing." *Biblical Archaeology Review*. March-April, pp. 24, 76.

Person Index (of the various genres cited)

Abbey, Mepkin	12
Ackerman Link, Julie	104, 155
Amstutz, Lisa J.	156
Angel, Chris	49
Athenogenes	12
Avery-Quash, Susanna	155
Bach, J. S.	127
Bainton, Roland	129
Baker, Henry W.	10
Barber, Samuel	19
Boers, Arthur	19, 155
Brenneman, Diane Zaerr	104, 155, 165, 167, 169, 177
Briggs, Jacky	107, 172, 181
Brodie, Thomas	93-95, 155, 164, 166, 171, 177, 179
Brumbaugh, Wilbur E.	45
Burge, Gary	80, 155, 175
Burkholder, Byron Rempel (see Rempel)	
Calvin, John	5
Cash, Johnny	19
Coloe, Mary L.	97, 155
Cookson, F. B.	110
Dali, Salvador	129, 155
Day, Janeth Norfleet	37, 155
de Maineri, Gian Francesco	129
Derstine, M. Gerald (see Martin, JD)	
de Waal, Esther	51, 164, 174
Dowd, Brother James	132-33, 165, 172, 175, 178
Dueck, Paul	99, 166, 180
Dustin, Patricia Snyder	53
Edwards, Mark	137, 155
Elderkin, George D.	53
Ellul, Jacques	7, 155, 163, 180
Epp Miller, Rachel	80, 164, 175
Fecher, Michael	158
Finaldi, Gabriela	129, 155
Foley, John B.	49, 166, 179, 180
Fox, George	62, 155, 165, 174, 178
Freeman, Arthur	75-76, 156, 164, 165, 171, 174, 177, 181
Funk, Joseph	135
Gérard, Max	155
Gibson, Mel	129
Graber, Brent	18, 182

Graham, Billy	5
Grubb, Mary	129
Grün, Anselm	69, 156, 166, 169
Grünewald, Mathis	129
Hall, Eddy	95, 103, 156, 166, 172, 179
Herr, Gene	181
Hershberger, Martha	53
Hildegard, of Bingen	2, 9, 157, 164, 165, 179
Hittinger, Russell	129
Hubmaier, Balthasar	42-43, 156
Hunt, William Holman	127
Jackson, Donald	14, 15
Jackson, Gwen	136
Jasper, Alison	9, 156
Johns, Loren	157
Kasper, Cardinal Walter	156
Katongole, Emmanuel	86, 156
Kauffman, Ivan J.	61, 156
Kauffman, Lloyd	110
Kauffman, Richard	103
King, Martin Luther	91
Klassen, Mary E.	154, 181, 182
Krabill, James R.	157
Kreider, Eleanor	121, 156, 165, 167, 176, 177, 178
Kropf, Marlene	9, 95, 103, 109, 156, 166, 172, 173, 179
Kulp, Judith Baer	156
Kurth, Willi	156
Landis, Susan Mark	92, 102, 133, 156-57, 164, 171, 178
Langmuir, Erika	129, 157
Lev, Elizabeth	129
Link, Julie Ackerman	104
Longley, Jim	148-49, 165, 167, 173
Longley, Sally	149-51, 163, 165, 167, 173, 181
Longfellow, Samuel	135
Lund, Andrew	55
Luther, Martin	5
Lytle, Kirk & Patty	88, 182
MacArthur, Neil	155
MacGregor, Neil	129, 157
McFadden, Rosanna Eller	Cover art, i
Mark, Arlene	22, 90, 157, 171, 175
Martin, JD (M. Gerald. Derstine)	49, 166, 174, 179, 180
Meacham, John	132

Meade, Pachomius	v, 72, 178, 181
Mishler, John	118-19, 181
Morse, Eleanor R.	155
Morse, Kenneth .	45, 165, 170, 174
Mostaert, Jan	129
Mother Teresa	5
Mullins, Rich	98, 166, 180
Murray, Shirley Erena	110
Nafziger, Kenneth	28, 95
Neale, John M.	10
Neff, David	129
Neuls-Bates, Carol	2, 157
Palmezzano, Marcos	129
Park, Andy	99
Peter, Galen A.	157
Pipkin, Wayne	156
Plummer, Christopher	22, 130
Prudentius, Aurelius Clemens	10, 171
Rempel-Burkholder, Byron	102, 163, 167, 175, 180
Rice, Chris	86, 156
Rohr, Richard	126-27, 157, 164, 171, 176, 177
Rossé, Gerard	115, 157, 164, 175, 178, 179, 181
Roth, Willard E.	22, 166, 175, 180, 181
Schmidt, Orlando	157
Shenk, David W.	157
Shenk, Jen Helmuth	23-25, 29, 55-59, 119, 163, 170, 174, 175, 176, 178, 181, 182
Shenk, Kris A.	28-29, 154, 181
Shenk, Shirley A.,	111-12, 181
Siemens, Lois	34, 165, 172, 176, 180
Short, Pam Graf	4-6, 165, 169, 171, 173, 175, 180
Simms, Darin	i, 182
Sink, Susan	14, 157
Snider, Cindy	156
Snodgrass, Fred	143
Snyder, C. Arnold	157
Snyder Belousek, Darrin	106, 166, 169, 171, 172, 175
Stover, Gerald	181
Swartley, Libby	108, 163, 169, 175, 181
Swartley, Willard M.	3, 18, 46, 50, 54, 105, 122, 143-48, 152, 156-57 (wms) passim in Topic Index
Talbot, John Michael	10, 19, 26, 43, 165, 170, 173, 174, 176, 180, 182

Tanner, Henry D.	27
Teel, Jim	99
Teng, Kuaying	66-67
Tice, Adam	13, 35-36, 49, 77, 166, 171, 172, 173, 174, 175, 176, 177, 179, 180, 181
Toolan, Sarah	44, 165, 170, 174, 177, 179
Van Dyck, Anthony	129
Van Kaam, Adrian	8, 85, 116-17, 158, 163, 164, 169, 171, 172, 175, 179, 180
Vanier, Jean	2, 19, 42, 48, 114, 116, 117, 123, 158, 164, 170, 172, 175, 177, 179
Waring, Anna L.	70, 117
Weaver, Nigel	135, 177
Webber, Robert E.	158
Weems, Ann	131, 158, 165, 177
Wenger, J. C.	134
Wheeler, Maritz	158
Witherington, Ben III	158
Wuellner, Flora Slosson	103
Yoder, John H.	156

Index by Genre

Art

Cover:	Light of Christ Panels, Rosanna Eller McFadden	i
Figure 1	*"Word Made Flesh"*—Donald Jackson, *The Saint John's Bible*	14-15
Figure 2	Nicodemus, Henry O. Tanner	27
Figure 3	"Transformation" Mosaic, by Kris A. Shenk	28-29
Figure 4	Jesus and the Samaritan Woman, Websites	37
Figure 5	Jesus heals the blind man, Websites	65
Figure 6a	Jesus the Good Shepherd (websites)	71
Figure 6b	Jesus the Good Shepherd (Pachomius Meade)	72
Figure 7	Martha: "I believe you are the Messiah (website)	78
Figure 8a	Enactment of the Last Supper (Bahia Vista photo)	88
Figure 8b	Jesus washes his disciples' feet (Bahia Vista photo)	89
Figure 9a	The Vine and the Branches (Jacky Briggs)	107
Figure 9b	Abide in My Love, by Libby Swartley	108
Figure 10	Peace on Earth, by Shirley A. Shenk	111-12
Figure 11a	The Cross (John Mishler, sculptor)	119
Figure 11b	Unity for all Believers (Ten Thousand Villages)	120
Figure 12	"Resurrection" Batik, Gwen Jackson	136
Figure 13	Mary Magdalene and the Risen Jesus (websites)	137
Figure 14	Thomas Encounters the Risen Lord (websites)	139
Figure 15	Antiphon Calligraphy (Sally Longley)	149-51
Figure 16	"Journey" (Kris A. Shenk)	154

Confession

Power of Love (Byron Rempel-Burkholder)	102

Drama

Jesus and Nicodemus (Jen Helmuth Shenk)	23-25
Jesus and the Samaritan Woman (wms)	32-33
Jesus heals the blind man (Jen Helmuth Shenk)	55-59
Jesus and Simon Peter (wms)	142

Meditation (blends with poetry, song, and art)

On the Prologue

Jacques Ellul	7
Adrian van Kaam	8

Willard Swartley	8
Hildegard of Bingen	9
On Calling and Discipleship (wms)	19
On John 3:16 (wms)	26
Light piercing darkness (wms/Talbot)	26
Divine and Medical in Healing (wms)	39-40
On Jesus as Bread of Life	
B. Hubmaier	42
J. Vanier	42
John 7:37 and Matthew 11:28 (Vanier)	48
"Transfiguration" (de Waal)	51
Garment of Light (wms/de Waal)	51
Images of Jesus (Anselm Grün)	69
Songs on Jesus as Good Shepherd (wms)	70
Lazarus (Arthur Freeman)	75-76
Lazarus's death (Adam Tice)	77
Jesus Palm Sunday Entry (wms)	79
Greeks come: My hour has come (wms)	79-80
Greeks' inquiry and Mennonites (Rachel Epp Miller)	80
Responses to Jesus (wms)	80-81
Jesus' Self-giving and Glory (Adrian van Kaam)	85
Reconciliation through footwashing (wms)	85-86
Songs on Footwashing (wms)	86-87
Songs on Love (wms)	87
The rent we pay for living (Susan Mark Landis)	91-92
Spiritual Formation (Brodie)	93-95
My Father's House (wms)	97
Relation to Jesus the Vine (wms)	103
Abiding and Bearing Fruit (wms)	103
Friendship (John 15:12) (Julie Ackerman Link)	104
Our Needs; Jesus' *I Am*s (wms)	105
Holy Spirit/Paraclete (wms)	109-110
John 17 (Jean Vanier)	114-15
John 17:17-23 (Gerard Rossé)	115
Love and Unity (Jean Vanier)	116
Unity and Trinity (Adrian van Kaam)	116-17
Peter (Jean Vanier)	123-24
Jesus' *I thirst* (wms)	125-26

Jesus as scapegoat (Richard Rohr)   126-27
Pilate's Cross Inscription (wms)   127
John's Passion in Art and Song (wms)   129-30
He breathed on them (James Dowd)   132-33
Peace (Menno Simons)   134
Peter's Healing of Memories (wms)   143-47
John's *Word* and *I AM*s (Jim & Sally Longley)   148-51

Poetry (entries under **Song/Hymn** fit here also)
    Prologue: Song of Invitation and Grace (Pamela Graf Short)   4-6
        Highest and fiery power (Hildegard of Bingen)   9
    On Samaritan Woman (Lois Siemens)   34
    The Man Born Blind (Ivan Kauffman)   60-61
    Now the Lord has opened to me (George Fox)   62
    On Lazarus (Arthur Freeman)   75-76
    On Easter (Ann Weems)   131

Prayer
    On Abiding (Diane Zaerr Brenneman)   104
    For Protection (wms)   115
    For Love and Unity (Eleanor Kreider)   121
    Spiritual Reflection: Prayer (wms)   122

Sermon/Story
    Disability and Weakness (wms)   66-67
    On Footwashing (wms)   90
    On Pruning to yield fruit (wms)   103
    Peter: Standing by the Fire (wms)   143-47

Song/Hymn Titles
    A traveler unknown to me (Adam Tice)   35-36
    A woman poured her jar of rich perfume (Adam Tice)   77
    At the Name of Jesus (*HWB* 342)   40
    Bread of Life (John Michael Talbot)   43
    Bread of Life (*HWB* 455, Morse and Burmbaugh)   45
    Come and be light for our eyes (*SJ* 5)   63
    Come and see (*HWB* 20)   19
    Come, my Way, my Truth, my Life (*HWB* 587)   98-99

Don't be afraid (*SJ* 105)	110
Father/Jesus/Spirit, we adore you	40
Gentle Shepherd, come and lead us (*HWB* 352)	70
He Came Down (*SJ* 31)	86
Holy Spirit, truth divine (*SS* 105 and *HWB* 508)	135
I Am the Bread of Life (*HWB* 472, Sarah Toolan)	44
I AM the Living Water (Adam Tice)	49
In heavenly love abiding (*HWB* 613)	70
Jesus, Be the Center (*SS* 31)	52
Jesus is the True Vine (Snyder Belousek)	106
Jesus, Rock of Ages (*JD Martin, HWB 515*)	49
Jesus, the Light of the World (Elderkin)	53
Jesus, took a towel (*HWB* 449)	87
Light Eternal (John Michael Talbot)	10, 19, 26, 43
Listen, God is calling (*SJ* 42)	19
Longing for Light (*SJ* 54)	52
Loving Spirit (*SJ* 34)	110
My Shepherd will supply my need (*HWB* 589)	70
O Joyous Light of Glory (2nd century, *SJ* 116)	12
O let all who thirst (John B. Foley, *HWB* 495)	48-49
O Love of God (*HWB* 326)	86
O Power of love (*HWB* 593)	86
O Sacred Head now wounded (*HWB* 252)	127
Of the Father's Love Begotten (4th century)	11
One Thing I Ask (Andy Park)	99
Open my eyes, that I may see (*HWB* 517)	63
Praise/Adoring songs (wms/*HWB* 106-127)	40
Ride on, ride on in majesty (*HWB* 239)	81
Savior, like a shepherd lead us (*HWB* 355)	70
Spirit of God! descend (*HWB* 502)	95
That where I am, you may also be (Rich Mullin)	98
The church's one foundation (HWB 311)	117
The Glory of the Living Son (Adam Tice)	13
The King of Glory (Sing and Rejoice 122)	81-82
The Lord is my Shepherd (Paul Dueck)	99
The Lord's my shepherd (*HWB* 578 and *SS* 99)	70
The Risen Christ (SS 101)	135
Were you there? (*HWB* 257)	128
Unity (Gerald Derstine/JD Martin, *SR* 129)	117

When Jesus learned his friend had died (Adam Tice)   77

Spiritual Reflection(s)

    Thomas Brodie   93-95

    Marlene Kropf and Eddy Hall   103

    Willard Swartley   3, 18, 46, 50, 54, 122, 152

    Jim & Sally Longley (Antiphon)   148-51

Worship Resources (all the above, and specifically):

    Art: "Transformation" (Kris A. Shenk)   29

        "Journey" (Kris A. Shenk)   154

    Call to Worship (Willard Roth)   22

    Confession: Power to Love (Byron Rempel-Burkholder)   102

    Prayer: On Abiding (Diane Zaerr Brenneman)   104

    Prayer: God of love (*SJ* 121)   87

    Responsive Reading: Footwashing and Love (Arlene Mark)   90

    Jesus Prayer for his disciples (Eleanor Kreider)   121

    Benediction: Peace and Spirit: John 20:21-22   153
            (Eleanor Kreider)

Subject/Topical Index

Abbreviations

HWB	*Hymnal: A Worship Book*
SJ	*Sing the Journey*
SR	*Sing and Rejoice*
SS	*Sing the Story*
(wms)	Book Author: *Living Gift*
	Nuggets, undesignated, are: (wms)

Abiding (in Jesus)
    Art: "Abide in my Love" (Libby Swartley)   108
    Meditation: John 15:4-9 (wms)   103 (#1)
        Abiding and bearing fruit (wms)   103 (#2)
        Union with God (wms)   103 (#3)
        Father's house, abiding (wms)   104 (#4)
    Nuggets: John 15   101
    Song: "Jesus is the True Vine" (Snyder Belousek)   106
    Prayer: "Abide" (Diane Zaerr Brenneman)   104
Baptism
    Meditation: Garment of Light (wms)   51
    Nuggets: Footwashing renews baptism   86
Belief/believe
    Art: Thomas's "My Lord, and my God"   139
    Nuggets: Polarity with unbelief   21
        "We have come to believe…"   31
        John 20: Disciples' Responses   131
    Poetry: "Prologue: invitation and grace" (Pamela Graf Short)   4-6
    Song: "I Am the Bread of Life" (*HWB* 472)   44
        "Bread of Life" (*HWB* 455)   45
Beloved Disciple
    Meditation: Query: Is Lazarus an Author?   74
        Coupled with Love Command   85
    Nuggets: First identified at the Last Supper   85

        Enters High Priest Courtyard   123
        Jesus assigns his mother's care to him   125
        Races with Peter to the tomb   131, 125

Is the first to believe		131, 125
Among the seven disciples (21:2)		141
Sermon: At the table of the Lord's Supper		144
Peter trusts the Beloved Disciple		146
Spiritual Reflection: To embody his model (wms)		152
Birth (new)		
Art: Nicodemus Visiting Jesus		27
Drama: "Born from Above" (Jen Helmuth Shenk)		23-25
Blind (see Sight)		
Bread (of Life)		
Meditation: Jesus as Bread of Life		
Balthasar Hubmaier		42
Jean Vanier		42
Nuggets: Jesus as bread of life		41
Song: "The Bread of Life" (John Michael Talbot)		43
"I Am the Bread of Life" (Toolan, *HWB* 472)		44
"Bread of Life" (Morse, *HWB* 455)		45
Spiritual Reflection (wms)		46
Calling		
Drama: Jesus and Peter (wms)		142
Nuggets/Sermon: Jesus' First Disciples		17
Peter's Calling		141, 146
Song: "Come and see" (*HWB* 20)		19
"Listen, God is calling" (*SJ* 42)		14
Christmas (in John)		
Meditation: Willard Swartley		8
Christology (who is Jesus?) (implicitly *everything*!)		
Art: Jesus and the Samaritan Woman		37
Jesus Heals the Blind Man		65
Drama: "The Man Born Blind" (Jen Helmuth Shenk)		55-59
Jesus and Samaritan Woman (wms)		32-33
Meditation on John 5		40(#2-3)
Nuggets: The Prologue		7
John 1:19-51		17
John 5		39
Song: "I am the Bread of Life" (Sarah Toolan, *HWB* 472)		44
Spiritual Reflection (wms)		50

Creation (incl. new creation)

    See all entries under "Word/*Logos*" Nuggets: "

    Week of New Creation   17

    Poetry: "Prologue: invitation and grace" (Pamela Graf Short) 4-6

    Song: *Of the Father's Love Begotten*

            (Aurelius Clemens Prudentius) (*HWB* 104)   10-11

Death and Dying

    Meditation: on Lazarus' death (Adam Tice)   77

           Passion Art (wms)   129-30

           The sacrificed Lamb of God (Rohr)   126-27

           John's Passion in Art and Song (wms)   127-28

    Nuggets: Jesus' "Gethsemane" *hour* has come   79

    Poetry: Lazarus (Arthur Freeman)   75-76

    Song: Lyrics on Lazarus death (Adam Tice)   77

Discipleship

    Drama: Jesus and Simon Peter (wms)   142

    Meditation: Following Jesus   19 (#3)

           With Whom Do We Identify (wms)   80-81

           Peter's healing of memories (wms)   143-47

           John 13—17 (Brodie)   93-95

    Nuggets: John 1:19-51   17

           John 21   141

    Song: "Come and see" *HWB* 20   19

           "Jesus is the True Vine" (Snyder Belousek) 106

Faith Formation (see also "Belief" and "Discipleship")

    Drama: Jesus and Simon Peter (wms)   142

    Meditation: Disciplines for faith formation (wms)   19 (#2)

           Peter's healing of memories   143-47

           John 13—17 (Brodie)   93-95

    Spiritual Reflection: Response to Gospel (wms)   3, 152

Footwashing

    Art: Jesus washes his disciples' feet   89

    Meditation:

           Jesus' self-giving (Adrian van Kaam)   85 (#1)

           Hymns on Foot-washing   86-87

           "The rent we pay..." (Susan Mark Landis) 91-92

    Nuggets: Jesus washes his disciples' feet   85

    Responsive Reading: Footwashing (Arlene Mark)   90

Song:	"He came down" (*SJ* 31)	86 (#2)
	"He knelt down…" (*wms*)	86
	"Jesus took a towel" (*HWB* 449)	87 (#4)
Stories:	Footwashing at Lausanne	85-86
	Footwashing Practice (wms)	90

Forgiveness (see also Life, eternal)
"Holy Week" (Dowd)		132-33
Meditation: Hymns on footwashing		86-87(#3)
Nuggets: John 20		131
Song: "The Bread of Life" (Talbot)		43

Friendship
Nuggets: On John 15		101
Meditation: Jean Vanier		19 (#1)
	Spiritual Friendships (wms)	19 (#2)
	Friendship (Ackerman Link)	104 (#4)

Fruit-bearing
Art: Vine and branches (Jacky Briggs)	107
Meditation: #2 (from Kropf and Hall)	104
Nuggets: Central Emphases of John 15	102
Song: "Jesus is the True Vine" (Snyder Belousek)	106
Story: Apples and Blackberries	103

Gift (of God)
Art: Jesus and the Samaritan Woman	37
Drama: Jesus and Samaritan Woman (wms)	32-33

Glory/Glorify
Meditation: Hidden Glory (van Kaam)		85
Nuggets: Jesus' works glorify God		39
	Lazarus' death, to show God's glory	74
	Jesus' glorification *hour* has come	80
	Mutual glorification of Father and Son	83, 113
Song: O Joyous Light of Glory (*SJ* 116)		12
	"King of Glory" (*SR* 122)	47

God/Christ-Messiah/Spirit (almost everything, but "choice"
       entries below; includes Christology)
Art: Thomas's "My Lord, and my God"	139
Drama: Jesus and Samaritan Woman (wms)	32-33
Meditation: Praise Songs (wms)	40
Poetry: "Reflection" (Lois Siemens)	34

	Song: "A traveler unknown to me" (Adam Tice)	35-36
Grace		
	Poetry: "Prologue: Song of invitation and grace"	
	Pamela Graf Short	4-6
Healing		
	Art: Jesus Heals the Blind Man (artist unknown)	65
	Meditation: Divine and Medical in Healing (wms)	39-40
	Nuggets: The Nobleman's Son, 4:45-54	31
	The Lame Man at the Pool, 5:1-16	39
	Song: "The Bread of Life" (Talbot)	43
	Spiritual Reflection (wms)	46, 50
	Story: "Disability and Witness"	66-67
Hunger		
	Song: "I Am the Bread of Life" (*HWB* 472)	44
I AM (absolute)		
	Art: Jesus and the Samaritan Woman (artist unknown)	37
	Drama: Jesus to the Samaritan Woman (wms)	32-33
	Meditation: The "I AMs" of John's Gospel	
	(Jim & Sally Longley)	148-51
	Nuggets: Jesus' reveals self to Samaritan Woman	31
I AM (with predicate nominative)		
	Meditation: Jesus' seven I AMs and our needs (wms)	103
	The "I AMs" of John's Gospel	
	(Jim & Sally Longley)	148-51
	Song: "I Am the Bread of Life" (*HWB* 472)	44
	"Come my Way, my Truth, my Life" (*HWB* 587)	98-99
	"I AM the Living Water" (Adam Tice)	49
Incarnation		
	Art: "Word Made Flesh" (Donald Jackson)	14-15
	Meditation: Word became flesh (wms)	8 (#4)
	God in time and space (Marlene Kropf)	9 (#5)
	Nuggets: Word made flesh	7
Joy		
	Meditation on Song: "He came down..." (wms)	86
	Nuggets: Joy at heart of chiasm on John 15 (wms)	101
Lamb of God		
	Song: "In the Beginning" (in *Light Eternal* Talbot)	19

"Agnus Dei"(Samuel Barber)   19
"The Bread of Life" (in *Light Eternal*, Talbot)   43
Spiritual Reflection (wms)   50
Life (eternal)
    Art: Martha's Confession   78
    Drama: "Born from Above" (Jen Helmuth Shenk)   23-25
        Jesus and Samaritan Woman (wms)   32-33
    Nuggets: On Lazarus (wms)   73
    Poetry: "Prologue: invitation and grace" (Pamela Graf Short) 4-6
    Lazarus' resurrection (Arthur Freeman)   75-76
    Song: "When Jesus learned his friend had died" (A. Tice) 77
        "Jesus, Rock of Ages" (JD Martin)   49
        "Come, my way" (*HWB* 587)   98-99
    Spiritual Reflection: Life to humankind (wms)   10
        "Response to Gospel" (wms)   3, 152
Light
    Art: Jesus Heals the Blind Man   65
    Meditation: Jesus the Light (wms)   #s 1, 2, 3 on 52-53
        Light Eternal (Talbot)   10
        "Transfiguration" (de Waal)   51
    Nuggets: Polarity with darkness   8, 21
        Lights at Tabernacles   47
        "I am the light of the world"   51
    Poetry: "Prologue: invitation and grace" (Pam Graf Short) 4-6
        "Now the Lord has Opened to Me" (Fox)   62
        "The Man Born Blind" (Kauffman)   60-61
    Song: "O Joyous Light of Glory"   12
        Light Eternal (Talbot)   10-11, 26
        "Longing for Light" (*SJ* 54)   52
        "Jesus, be the center" (*SS* 31)   52
        "Jesus, the Light of the World"   53
        "Open my eyes, Lord" (*HWB* 517)   63
        "Come and be light for our eyes" (*SJ* 5)   63
    Spiritual Reflection: Jesus the Light (wms)   18, 46
        Response to Gospel (wms)   3, 152
Lord's Supper
    Nuggets: Jesus as Bread of Life   41
    Song: "The Bread of Life" (Talbot)   43

"I Am the Bread of Life" (Toolan, *HWB* 472)   44

"Bread of Life" (Morse, *HWB* 455)   45

Love

    Art: "Abide in My Love" (Libby Swartley)   108

    Call to Worship (Willard Roth)   22

    Confession (Byron Rempel-Burkholder)   104

    Drama: "Born from Above," Jen Helmuth Shenk   23-25

    Jesus and Simon Peter (wms)   142

    Meditation: God's love (wms)   11 (#1)

        Jean Vanier on 7:37   48

        Love and Unity (Vanier)   116 (#4)

        Love and Unity (van Kaam)   116-17 (#5)

        Peter's healing of memories   143-47

    Nuggets: Jesus' love commandment   93

    Poetry: "Prologue: invitation and grace" (Pamela Graf Short)   4-6

    Songs: "O Love of God" (*HWB* 326)   86

        "O Power of love" (*HWB* 593)   86

        "In heavenly love abiding" (Waring)   86

        "Jesus is the True Vine" (Snyder Belousek)   106

Love one another (recurring theme in last half of John)

    Call to Confession (Rempel-Burkholder)   102

    Nuggets: Love command with other themes 85, 93, 101, 113, 141

    Meditation

        Unity of Father and Son in love (Vanier)   116 (#5)

        Mutual love of Father and Son (van Kaam)   116-17 (#6)

        Song: "God of love" (*SJ* 121)   87

        "He came down that we may have love" (*SJ* 31)   87

        "A Woman poured her jar of rich perfume" (A.Tice)   77

        "Spirit of God! descend"   95

    Responsive Reading: On Footwashing and Love (A. Mark)   90

    Spiritual Reflection: Response to Gospel (wms)   3, 152

Mission

    Art: Jesus and the Samaritan Woman   37

    Call to Worship (Willard Roth)   22

    Drama: Jesus and Samaritan Woman (wms)   32-33

    Meditation: Sanctification, Mission, Unity (Gerard Rossé)   115

Greeks come to see Jesus (Burge; Epp Miller)	80
"Holy Week" (Dowd)	132-33
Forgiveness, mission, and peace (wms)	134 (#2)
Nuggets: Jesus' Goes through Samaria	31
Greeks come to see Jesus	79
Poetry: "Reflection" (Lois Siemens)	34
Song: A Traveler unknown to me (Adam Tice)	35-36
Spiritual Reflection: Response to Gospel (wms)	3, 152

Nicodemus

Art: Nicodemus (Henry O. Tanner)	27
Drama: "Born From Above" (Jen Helmuth Shenk)	23-25
Nuggets: Queries Jesus at night (3:1-12)	21
Objects to Plot of Council against Jesus	47
Anoints Jesus for burial	73
Song: *Light Eternal* in Meditation (wms/Talbot)	26 (#2)

Passion (Jesus')

Meditation:	
The sacrificed Lamb of God (Rohr)	126-27
John's Passion in Art and Song (wms)	129-30
Nuggets: Jesus' "Gethsemane" *hour* has come	79
Jesus' Trial and Death	125

Peace/Peacemaking

Art: Jesus and the Samaritan Woman (artist unknown)	37
Quilt Depiction: "Peace on Earth" (Shirley A. Shenk)	111-12
Benediction: John 20:21-22 (Eleanor Kreider)	153
Drama: Jesus and Samaritan Woman (wms)	32-33
Meditation: "Menno on Peace"	134
Greeks come to see Jesus	80
Forgiveness, mission, and peace (wms)	134 (#2)
"Holy Week" (Dowd)	132-33
Nuggets: Jesus' Goes through Samaria	31
Jesus promises peace	109
John 20	121
Poetry: "Reflection" (Lois Siemens)	34
Song: "A traveler unknown to me" (Adam Tice)	35-36
"The Bread of Life" (Talbot)	43
Spiritual Reflection: prayer (wms)	122

Peter

Calling		17, 141
Confession		41
Drama: Jesus and Simon Peter (wms)		142
Meditation: Peter's healing of memories (wms)		143-47
Nuggets: "You are the Holy One of God"		41
	Threefold Denial	123
	Restoration (21:15-17)	131
Sermon: "Standing by the Fire" (wms)		143-47
Prayer (praying)		
Meditation: Jesus prays to his Father (Vanier)		114-15
	Jesus' High Priestly Prayer	114-15
	"Praying with the Anabaptists"	103 (#2)
Nuggets: Themes in Farewell Discourse		93
Prayers: On Abiding (Diane Zaerr Brenneman)		104
	On Love and Unity (Eleanor Kreider)	121
	Pentecost: Receive the Spirit	100
Spiritual Reflection: Prayer (wms)		122
Protection		
Meditation: Protection Prayer (wms)		115 (#3)
	On John 13—17 (Brodie)	93-95
Prayer: Spiritual Reflection (wms)		122
Resurrection		
Art:	Martha's Confession (artist unknown)	78
	"Resurrection" Batik (Gwen Jackson)	136
	Mary Magdalene and Risen Jesus (artist unknown)	137
Meditation: "Holy Week" (Dowd)		132-33
Nuggets: Jesus raises believers on the last day		40
	On John 11	73
	On Lazarus	73
	On John 20	131
Poetry:	Lazarus (Arthur Freeman)	75-76
	"Easter" (Weems)	131
Song:	"I Am the Bread of Life" (Sarah Toolan, *HWB* 472)	44
	"When Jesus learned his friend had died" (A. Tice)	78
	"The Risen Christ" (*SS* 101, Nigel Weaver)	135
Salvation (see also Life, eternal)		
Meditation:		
	The sacrificed Lamb of God (Rohr)	126-27

John's Passion in Art and Song (wms)   130-31
Nuggets: Savior of the world, John 4   21
Sanctification (holiness)
    Meditation: #2 with Mission and Unity (Rossé)   115
    Nuggets: John 17   113
    Spiritual Reflection: John 17 (wms)   122
See/Sight
    Art: Jesus Heals the Blind Man (artist unknown)   65
    Drama: "The Man Born Blind" (Jen Helmuth Shenk)   55-59
    Poetry: "Now the Lord has Opened to Me" (Fox)   62
       "The Man Born Blind" (Kauffman)   61-62
    Song: "Open my eyes, Lord" (*HWB* 517)   63
       "Come and be light for our eyes" (*SJ* 5)   63-64
    Spiritual Reflection (wms)   50
Serve/Service
    Meditation: "The rent we pay..." (Susan Mark Landis)   92-93
    Nuggets: Footwashing and service   85
    Story: Footwashing Practice (wms)   90
Shepherd (Good/True/Beautiful)
    Art: Pastoral Scene (artist unknown)   71
    Icon (Pachomius Meade)   72
    Meditation:
       On Hymns (*HWB* 352, 355, 578;
       SS 99; Stanza 2-3 of *HWB* 613   70 (#1)
       Images of Jesus (Grün)   69 (#2)
Sin(s)
    Meditation: On Footwashing (wms)   52 (#3)
       Jesus' great commission (Dowd)   132-33
       Forgiveness, mission, and peace (wms)   134 (#2)
    Nuggets: Footwashing, forgiving sin(s)   85
    Song: "The Bread of Life" (Talbot)   43
    Story: Footwashing Practice (wms)   90
    Spiritual Reflection (wms)   152
Spirit (Holy)/Paraclete (see also God/Christ/Spirit)
    Benediction: John 20:21-22 (Eleanor Kreider)   153
    Meditation: Holy Spirit/Paraclete (wms)   109-10
       "Holy Week" (Dowd)   132-33
    Nuggets: Paraclete/Holy Spirit   109

Song: "Holy Spirit, Truth Divine" (*HWB* 508)   135
Spiritual Reflections: Grateful for Spirit (wms)   50
Prayer: Pentecost: Receive the Spirit (*SS* 189)   100
Prayer (wms)   122
Response to Gospel (wms)   3, 152
Spiritual Formation
   Meditation: "Farewell Discourse" (Thomas Brodie)   93-95
      On John 15 (Marlene Kropf & Eddy Hall)   95 (#2)
   Spiritual friendships/spiritual direction   19 (#2)
Thirst
   Drama: Jesus and Samaritan Woman (wms)   23-25
   Meditation: "I thirst" (wms)   125 (#1)
      Jean Vanier on 7:37   48 (#1)
   Song: A traveler unknown to me (Adam Tice)   35-36
      "I Am the Bread of Life" (Sarah Toolan, *HWB* 472)   44
      "O let all who thirst" (John B. Foley, *HWB* 495)   48-49
   Spiritual Reflection: Grateful (wms)   50
Triumph
   Meditation: "Trumphal Entry" (wms)   79 (#1)
   Nuggets: Jesus enters Jerusalem   79
   Song: "Ride on, ride on" (*HWB* 239)   81
      "King of Glory" (*SR* 122)   81-82
Unity
   Art: "Unity, for all believers"   120
   Drama: Jesus and Samaritan Woman (wms)   32-33
   Meditation: Love and Unity (Jean Vanier)   116 (#5)
      Love and Unity (Adrian van Kaam)   116(#6)
      Sanctification, Mission, Unity (Rossé)   115 (#3)
   Nuggets: Jesus' Peace Mission into Samaria   31
   Song: "Unity" (JD Martin; Gerald Derstine; *SR* 129)   117
      "The Church's one foundation" (*HWB* 311)   117
Water
   Art: Jesus and the Samaritan Woman (website)   37
   Drama: "She came to draw water" (wms)   32-33
   Meditation: "Reflection" (Lois Siemens)   34
      "John 7:37 and Matthew 11:28" (Jean Vanier)   48
      "Our need, Jesus' promise" (wms)   104-5 (#6)
   Nuggets: Jesus promises living water   31

"Jesus: Living Water" at Tabernacles	47
Poetry: "Reflection" (Lois Siemens)	34
Song: "A traveler unknown to me" (Adam Tice)	35
"O let all who thirst" (John B. Foley; *HWB* 495)	48-49
"Rock of Ages" (JD Martin)	49
"I AM the Living Water" (Adam Tice)	49
Spiritual Reflection (wms)	50
Wedding (Bridegroom)	
Nuggets: Cana wedding	17
John as friend of bridegroom	21
Spiritual Reflection: Wedding (wms)	18
Wisdom (creation)	
Poetry: Hildegard of Bingen	10
Word/*Logos*	
Meditation: Jacques Ellul	7-8 (#1)
Van Kaam	8 (#2)
Poetry: "Prologue: invitation and grace" (Pamela Graf Short)	4-6
Song: "In the Beginning" (John Michael Talbot)	10
Of the Father's Love Begotten	10-11
Spiritual Reflection: wms	15
*Worship	
Art: "Transformation" (Kris A. Shenk)	28-29
Call to Worship (Willard Roth)	22
Confession (Byron Rempel-Burkholder)	102
Drama: Jesus and Samaritan Woman (wms)	32-33
Meditation: "My Father's House" (wms)	97 (1)
Nuggets: Jesus Goes through Samaria	31
Poetry: "Reflection" (Lois Siemens)	34
Song: "A traveler unknown to me" (Adam Tice)	35-36
Psalm 84 (Paul Dueck)	99
"In My Father's House" (Rich Mullins)	98

*These listed are on the topic of worship. Everything contributes to worship!

Acknowledgments

A number of entries are contributions of my Gospel of John students at Anabaptist Mennonite Biblical Seminary. In 2004 and 2006 students submitted expositions of selected texts. Often their papers concluded with a poetic response or spiritual reflection. Some ended with hymn compositions (note Adam Tice's contributions). From those initial gifts I have expanded the genres and entries. This book is a companion volume to the Believers Church Bible Commentary on John's Gospel that I authored.

Special thanks to Jen Shenk and Willard Roth who gave helpful counsel. Jen's suggestion of a "Nuggets" section heading each chapter bridges between this book and the Commentary. Jen persuaded me that a Genre index and a "Subject/Topical Index" would make the book helpful to pastors, teachers, and leaders of worship and song. Willard Roth's numerous helpful suggestions improve the book's aesthetic quality, e.g. consistency in style and simplifying what was originally more complex. Roth also read the volume with his keen editorial eye, and I am grateful. Gene Herr recommended Adrian van Kaam's book and Gerald Stover, Gerard Rossé's. Both greatly enrich this volume. For the poems on Lazarus by Arthur Freeman I am grateful to Gerald Stover for calling them to my attention. I thank both Gene and Gerald for other resources that enrich this volume and my BCBC Commentary as well.

For the art in this book I express special appreciation. Rosanna Eller McFadden's four-banner panel for the cover, together with Mary Klassen's photography, enhances this book laudably. Thank you to both. I am grateful indeed to *The Saint John's Bible* for permission to use the image, "Word Made Flesh" by Donald Jackson. Many thanks also to The Printery House for Figures 6b (Rev. Pachomius Meade, O.S.B) and 9a (Jacky Briggs). I am grateful also to Gwen Jackson for her batik "Resurrection" image. I thank Sally Longley for the lovely calligraphy of Jim's "Word / I AM" antiphon.

Nearer home are the stunning contributions of Kris A. Shenk, Shirley A. Shenk, and John Mishler. What a treasure! Heartfelt thanks! My fifteen year old granddaughter, Libby Swartley, with art in her wings, contributed a painting for John 15. Thank you, Libby.

I thank the photographers whose skill contributed much to this book: Jen Shenk, Leo Spillane, Mary Klassen, and Bruce Lehman who preserved the visuals for the drama, "A Night to Remember" (presented at Bahia Vista Mennonite Church under the direction of Kirk and Patti Lytle). These enrich this volume. Thank you *all* for permission to use these creative contributions. The art images from Google websites also contribute much, but in most cases I have not been able to locate the original source. If anyone knows these sources, please inform the author, so they can be acknowledged in any subsequent printing. For permission to use numerous song lyrics, notably John Michael Talbot's, "Poetry," and "Meditation" (including various genres from AMBS students), I am most grateful. Brent Graber, IT person at AMBS, has helped me through many computer vexations.

I thank Evangel Press for publishing this volume, especially Darin Simms who from the outset took keen interest in the volume. I am grateful to those who submitted endorsements for this book. Most important, I thank Mary, my wife, who read the manuscript numerous times, made good suggestions, and did copy editing.

Willard Swartley

Willard Swartley is Professor Emeritus at Anabaptist Mennonite Biblical Seminary in Elkhart, Indiana. He joined the faculty in 1978 and continued teaching until 2006. He served as Academic Dean at AMBS for seven years (1979-81; 1995-2001). Earlier he taught at Eastern Mennonite College nine years and Conrad Grebel College one year as visiting professor. He completed his Ph.D. in 1973 in New Testament (Princeton Theological Seminary). He began his teaching career at Goshen College/Biblical Seminary while serving as pastor of Locust Grove Mennonite Church (Elkhart, IN), where he was ordained in 1961.

His most recent books are *John* for the Believers Church Bible Commentary series (Herald Press, 2013); *Health, Healing and the Church's Mission* (InterVarsity Press, 2012); *Send Forth Your Light: A Vision for Peace, Mission, and Worship* (Herald Press, 2007); and *Covenant of Peace* (Eerdmans, 2006). He published several earlier books, including *Slavery, Sabbath, War, and Women* (Herald Press, 1983). He has edited over thirty books (ten as New Testament editor of the Believers Church Bible Commentary) and *Love of Enemy and Nonretaliation in the New Testament* (Westminster/John Knox Press, 1992; now available from editor Swartley), among others. In addition to many published articles he has four entries in Baker's *Dictionary on Scripture and Ethics* (2011) and six in *The Westminster Theological Wordbook of the Bible* (Westminster/John Knox Press, 2003). *Living Gift: John's Jesus in Meditation and Poetry, Art and Song* is his first book that incorporates various genres to foster spiritual formation.

Willard was the youngest in a family of eight children growing up on a farm near the Delaware River on the rolling hills of Bucks County, Pennsylvania. Willard and his wife Mary are actively involved in the Belmont Mennonite Church and are the parents of Louisa Swartley Oyer and Kenton Swartley, and grandparents of John and Michael Oyer, and Kristen, Jeremy, Libby and Michelle Swartley.